Sustainable Investment Policy Perspectives in the Economic Community of West African States (ECOWAS)

OECD

BETTER POLICIES FOR BETTER LIVES

Please cite this publication as:
OECD (2024), *Sustainable Investment Policy Perspectives in the Economic Community of West African States (ECOWAS)*, OECD Publishing, Paris, https://doi.org/10.1787/654e2de5-en.

ISBN 978-92-64-68158-3 (print)
ISBN 978-92-64-59488-3 (pdf)
ISBN 978-92-64-83025-7 (HTML)
ISBN 978-92-64-52044-8 (epub)

Photo credits: Cover © Jacek_Sopotnicki/Getty Images.

Corrigenda to OECD publications may be found on line at: www.oecd.org/about/publishing/corrigenda.htm.

Foreword

The recent African Continental Free Trade Agreement (AfCFTA) will offer both greater opportunities for ECOWAS Members within an integrated continental market as well as increased competition for footloose investment. This implies an even greater need to focus on raising the competitiveness of the region for sustainable investment.

This report is designed as a baseline diagnostic to explore ways to reinvigorate the reform of the ECOWAS investment climate while also providing a greater focus on how to improve sustainable outcomes from investment. The work is intended to point to areas where further collaboration between ECOWAS and the OECD could contribute to improved investment climates throughout the region.

The aim is not to provide a ready-made reform agenda for countries in the region but rather to explore policy areas which influence investment and its impact. The selection of topics is not all-encompassing, as it leaves out key issues such as the degree of discrimination against foreign investors contained in national legislation which can play an important role in FDI attraction. Further collaboration in this area could involve the inclusion of all ECOWAS Member States in the OECD FDI Regulatory Restrictiveness Index, a key measure of the extent of discrimination covering over 100 countries worldwide.

This report also provided background analysis for a public-private dialogue on Unlocking Investment for Sustainable Investment in ECOWAS, jointly hosted by ECOWAS and the OECD in Lomé, Togo on 11-12 May 2023. The dialogue aimed diagnose the weaknesses in the regional investment climate and to identify areas for future reforms, with the active engagement of policymakers from the region, as well as local and foreign businesses.

A companion report was also prepared for the Southern African Development Community (SADC), another important regional economic community in Africa. Given that the two regions are confronted with similar challenges in mobilising investment for sustainable development, as well as in fostering greater regional and continental integration, the two reports share a similar structure and analysis. Many of the recommendations are also common, given the parallel challenges and the high level of generality of this preliminary scoping report. These reports provide a solid basis for developing a long-term programme of collaboration with each region, using more tailor-made approaches based on the specificities of each region.

Table of contents

Foreword 3

Executive summary 6

1 Overview 9
- Key messages and considerations 15
- References 18

2 Rebalancing and aligning investment policy for sustainable development 21
- The international regime for investment protection is under increasing strain 22
- Treaty innovations at regional and continental level in Africa 23
- Investment laws of the ECOWAS member states 28
- References 33

3 Promoting sustainable investment 35
- Promoting and facilitating investment in ECOWAS 36
- How IPAs support the SDGs: experience from other regions 37
- Priority sectors and sustainability in ECOWAS 39
- Indicators to prioritise and measure sustainability outcomes of FDI 41
- References 43

4 Assessing use and design of investment incentives 45
- Investment tax incentives: opportunities and challenges 47
- Tax incentive design in ECOWAS: insights from the OECD ITID 49
- Assessing the impact of incentives: next steps 59

5 Promoting investment for green growth 67
- Green growth and climate change in West Africa 68
- Policy framework for green growth and climate change 73
- Policy approaches to promote green investment 77
- References 82

6 Promoting and enabling responsible business conduct 85
- Promoting RBC to drive trade, investment and sustainable development 86
- Promoting RBC in ECOWAS and its Member States 89
- References 95
- Annex 6.A. RBC related frameworks and initiatives 100

FIGURES

Figure 1.1. FDI flows are on a declining trend since 2011 11
Figure 1.2. FDI stocks are concentrated in Nigeria, Ghana, Côte d'Ivoire and Liberia 12
Figure 1.3. The EU represents the largest source of FDI in the ECOWAS region 12
Figure 1.4. Job intensity of FDI depends on economic structure and stage of development 13
Figure 1.5. FDI is an important driver of productivity and innovation 14
Figure 1.6. FDI in renewables has gained in importance in recent years 15
Figure 3.1. Main services provided by ECOWAS IPAs 37
Figure 3.2. Top factors motivating IPAs' current priorities in ASEAN and OECD countries 38
Figure 3.3. The SDGs to which IPAs in ASEAN and OECD contribute 39
Figure 3.4. Types of KPIs used for FDI prioritisation by ASEAN and OECD agencies 41
Figure 4.1. Income-based incentives are prevalent in ECOWAS 52
Figure 4.2. Most income-based incentives granted for 5-10 years, many are permanent 53
Figure 4.3. Nearly all incentives target certain sectors, most require multiple eligibility conditions 54
Figure 4.4. Sector-based incentives favour agriculture, manufacturing and services 55
Figure 4.5. Many incentives in ECOWAS support development goals 58
Figure 4.6. ECOWAS countries grant tax incentives through the Ministry of Finance but some countries grant incentives also through IPAs and other government bodies 59
Figure 5.1. Forest cover as a share of land area in ECOWAS, 1990-2020 69
Figure 5.2. Carbon emissions in West Africa 70
Figure 5.3. Resilience to climate change in ECOWAS 71
Figure 5.4. Electrification remains low in rural parts of West Africa 72
Figure 5.5. FDI in renewable energy is rising 72
Figure 5.6. Tax incentives continue to favour fossil fuels 80
Figure 6.1. The risk-based due diligence process and supporting measures 89

TABLES

Table 2.1. National investment laws in ECOWAS do not fully reflect broader continental approaches 33
Table 3.1. Main sectors promoted by ECOWAS IPAs 40
Table 5.1. Selected economic and environmental indicators 69
Table 5.2. Multilateral environmental agreements (MEAs) ratified by ECOWAS Member States 74
Table 5.3. NDC targets of ECOWAS Members 75
Table 5.4. Common elements of EIA systems in ECOWAS 76
Table 5.5. Financial support for renewable energy 78
Table 5.6. Technical and information support for green investments 81
Table 6.1. ECOWAS policy frameworks related to RBC 90
Table 6.2. Adherence/ Ratification of key international RBC-related frameworks in ECOWAS 93
Table 6.3. Development of National Action Plan on Business and Human Rights in ECOWAS 93

Executive summary

West Africa offers a large and diverse market of over 400 million people and natural resource wealth, yet it is not currently living up to its potential as a destination for international investment. Inflows of foreign direct investment (FDI) in the region have stagnated, in spite of some modest improvement in 2021. Furthermore, FDI in the region has not always fulfilled its promise in terms of promoting sustainable development. No single factor alone can explain this trend, but it strongly suggests that the region does not sufficiently provide a conducive environment for sustainable investment. Beyond political instability and strife, elements commonly cited within the region include fragmented regulatory frameworks, small market sizes, and insufficient infrastructure and skills.

In recognition of the challenge of attracting FDI to create jobs and promote sustainable development, the Member States of the Economic Community of West African States (ECOWAS) have taken steps to improve policies and governance in the region. This includes the ECOWAS Investment Policy, based in part on the OECD Policy Framework for Investment, whose primary purpose was to establish harmonised regional investment-climate policies. This framework is complemented by the ECOWAS Supplementary Investment Act and the ECOWAS Investment Code. These regional initiatives are intended to provide guidance for implementing country-level reforms.

This report is designed as a baseline diagnostic to explore ways to reinvigorate the reform of the ECOWAS investment climate while also providing a greater focus on how to improve sustainable outcomes from investment. This report looks primarily at what host governments can do to attract sustainable investment and promote the benefits of investment for social and environmental objectives, including how to facilitate and enable RBC. It provides an analysis to make ECOWAS a preferred destination for national and foreign investment that is reinforced by effective governance that promotes sustainable and inclusive regional economic development. It is based on the OECD tools, including the Policy Framework for Investment and the FDI Qualities Policy Toolkit and Indicators. Key messages and main considerations that emerge from the report are the following:

- *Increase coherence between national legislation and regional and continental treaties.* Greater coherence in approaches within and across regions in Africa at all levels could contribute to improved clarity and predictability for both governments and investors, although sufficient room should be left for further experimentation at national level.
- *Consider further integrating SDG considerations into investment promotion strategies of ECOWAS Member States.* IPAs in the region should increase focus on attracting FDI that contributes to the SDGs and prioritise investors with good sustainability track-records.
- *Further develop IPAs' value propositions for sustainable investment opportunities*. IPAs in the region should enhance their value propositions for sustainable investment opportunities by providing prospective investors with detailed and comprehensive legal and industry information, potentially also bankable projects, and improving their marketing.
- *Put in place adequate key performance indicators (KPIs) to ensure effective prioritisation and sound monitoring and evaluation by IPAs*. ECOWAS IPAs should also ensure that the KPIs used

to select priority investments and measure their outcomes are aligned with national development objectives and the agencies' overarching investment promotion priorities.

- *Use the SDGs to guide investment facilitation and aftercare services of IPAs to existing investors looking to expand or reinvest.* IPAs in ECOWAS could consider focusing aftercare activities on investors with the highest sustainability impacts, and encourage investors to comply with sustainability-related laws and to embrace responsible practices in their business operations.
- *Assess whether investment tax incentives are aligned with investment promotion strategies and SDGs, and consider whether they are the best policy instrument to achieve these goals*. Economic, social and environmental goals might be better supported by other policies, and tax incentives should be used in complement with wider development strategies.
- *Ensure that incentives are designed to generate investments that would not materialise otherwise*. Governments could consider phasing out costly profit-based incentives and introducing more targeted types of incentives. Improving incentive design, by promoting desired outcomes through tax relief on qualifying expenditure, can help limit redundancies and encourage positive spillovers.
- *Improve monitoring and evaluation of the costs, benefits and uptake of tax incentives.* The ECOWAS Commission could play an important role in advocating for improved monitoring and evaluation, as well as transparency and good governance in incentive policies.
- *Strengthen NDC targets and develop long-term low-emission development strategies.* Long-term strategies offer many benefits, including guiding countries to avoid costly investments in high-emissions technologies, supporting just and equitable transitions, and sending early and predictable signals to investors about envisaged long-term societal changes.
- *Use ECOWAS as a platform to promote strategic environmental assessments (SEA) and transboundary environmental impact assessment (EIA).* Recognition of transboundary SEA and EIA at the ECOWAS level could encourage other ECOWAS governments to adopt these tools in their national EIA systems.
- *Consider scaling down or phasing out investment incentives for non-green activities.* ECOWAS countries would benefit from classifying green and nongreen activities in targeted sectors using emerging taxonomies and scaling down or phasing out lengthy corporate-income tax holidays for non-green activities.
- *Consider developing frameworks for voluntary disclosure of environmental and climate impacts.* Frameworks for climate-related disclosure help to reveal how companies are preparing for a lower-carbon economy and support investors to better assess financial exposure to climate-related risks.
- *Raise awareness about the relevance and key elements of RBC.* ECOWAS and its Member States could strategically raise awareness and foster the understanding about the relevance of RBC in relation to trade and investment, through learning activities and workshops on international RBC instruments and risk-based due diligence.
- *Create an enabling environment to implement and enforce policies promoting RBC.* National governments could lead the way by developing and implementing National Action Plans on RBC as well as sector or issue-specific reforms.
- *Ensure policy coherence and harmonisation on RBC in line with international standards.* ECOWAS could support alignment and coordination of policies on RBC among Member States to ensure a common approach and level-playing field at the regional level.
- Build the capacity of companies to carry out due diligence. ECOWAS and its Member States could promote the use of the OECD due diligence framework by enterprises in ECOWAS and actively support the uptake of due diligence by companies, investors, and other stakeholders.

1 Overview

This chapter provides an overview of recent foreign direct investment (FDI) trends in ECOWAS, including a preliminary assessment of its contribution to sustainable development. It then summarises key messages and main considerations that emerge from the substantive chapters of the report.

Introduction

West Africa offers a large and diverse market of over 400 million people and natural resource wealth, yet it is not currently living up to its potential as a destination for international investment. Inflows of foreign direct investment (FDI) in the region have stagnated, whether in absolute terms or as a share of total FDI to Africa, in spite of some modest improvement in 2021. Furthermore, the investment the region has received has not always fulfilled its promise in terms of promoting sustainable development. No single factor alone can explain this trend but it strongly suggests that the region does not sufficiently provide a conducive investment climate for multinational enterprises (MNEs) to invest and create positive spillovers. Beyond political instability and strife, elements commonly cited within the region include fragmented investment and trade legal, regulatory and institutional frameworks, small market size in most countries in the region, and insufficient infrastructure and skilled labour (ECOWAS, 2018[1]).

The recent African Continental Free Trade Agreement (AfCFTA) will offer both greater opportunities for ECOWAS Members within an integrated continental market as well as increased competition for footloose investment. This will imply an even greater need to focus on raising the competitiveness of the region for investment.

In recognition of the challenge of attracting FDI to create jobs and promote sustainable development, the Member States of the Economic Community of West African States (ECOWAS) have taken steps to improve policies and governance in the region. This includes the ECOWAS Investment Policy (ECOWAS, 2018[1]), based in part on the OECD Policy Framework for Investment, whose primary purpose was to establish harmonised regional investment-climate policies. This framework is complemented by the ECOWAS Supplementary Investment Act and the ECOWAS Investment Code (ECOWAS, 2018[2]; 2008[3]). These regional initiatives are intended to provide guidance for implementing country-level reforms.

To provide greater impetus for reform and to showcase results, ECOWAS Member States also collaborated with the World Bank in an EU-funded project to develop an Investment Climate Scorecard, with six Member States involved in an initial pilot study. The competing demands on the scarce resources of governments involved in this work have made this project difficult to sustain half a decade after its inception.

This report is designed as a baseline diagnostic to explore ways to reinvigorate the reform of the ECOWAS investment climate while also providing a greater focus on how to improve sustainable outcomes from investment. The work is intended to point to areas where further collaboration between ECOWAS and the OECD could contribute to improved investment climates throughout the region.

The policy areas covered in this study include the national regulatory framework encapsulated in national investment laws and how this compares with initiatives at a regional level, investment promotion and facilitation in ECOWAS, investment incentives, investment for green growth and, lastly, responsible business conduct. The selection of areas builds on OECD work in these areas to highlight essential elements of a conducive investment climate which promotes not only FDI but also sustainable outcomes.

Recent trends in FDI in ECOWAS and estimates of its impact

The inflow of FDI to ECOWAS has been modest over the past 15 years. After a surge in inflows until 2008, FDI subsided during the global financial crisis and followed a downward trend until 2018 when FDI inflows reached 2006 levels (Figure 1.1, Panel A). Nigeria, the largest economy in ECOWAS, has seen an especially large decline in FDI inflows since 2011, when the security situation deteriorated in several parts of the country due to the rise of terrorist groups, cases of banditry and kidnappings, and separatist agitations (World Bank, 2023[4]). Other lower-middle income countries in the region (i.e. Benin, Cabo Verde, Côte d'Ivoire, Ghana and Senegal) have instead experienced increasing FDI inflows, at least until the onset of the COVID-19 pandemic. Zooming in on the number and size of cross-border investments in new physical projects or expansion of existing investments (i.e. greenfield FDI projects), shows that a resurgence of FDI inflows to ECOWAS in 2018 was abruptly interrupted by the outbreak of the Covid-19 pandemic and has not recovered thus far (Figure 1.1, Panel B).

Figure 1.1. FDI flows are on a declining trend since 2011

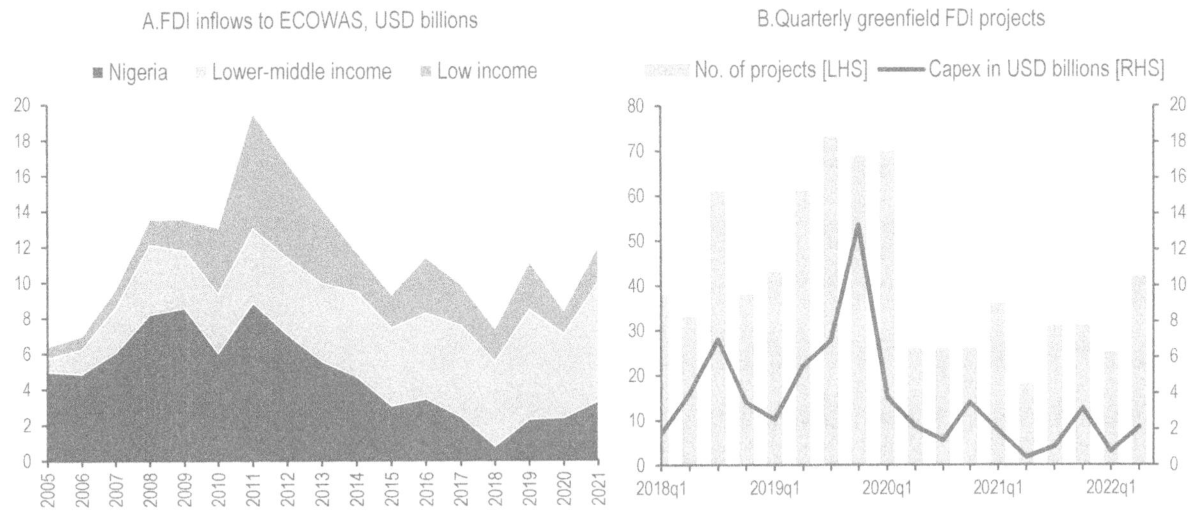

Note: Countries are grouped following the 2022 World Bank classification: Low income = Burkina Faso, Gambia, Guinea, Guinea-Bissau, Liberia, Mali, Niger, Sierra Leone, and Togo; lower-middle income = Benin, Cabo Verde, Côte d'Ivoire, Ghana, and Senegal. Panel B shows all opened and announced greenfield FDI projects between 2018 and 2022q2.
Source: OECD based on IMF Balance of Payments Statistics (2023[5]) and Financial Times fDi Markets Financial Times (2023[6])

The stock of FDI in West Africa is highly concentrated in Nigeria and is largely correlated with the economic size of countries in the region. At around US$ 91 billion, Nigeria hosts close to half of the region's FDI stock, followed by Ghana (21%), Côte d'Ivoire (6%), and Senegal (5%), which jointly account for one third of the FDI stock (Figure 1.2). A further 15% is accounted for by Liberia (5%), Niger (4%), Mali (3%), and Guinea (3%) while the remaining countries jointly account for around 7%. Although Liberia accounts for a relatively small share of the region's GDP of 0.5%, it hosts 5% of the region's FDI stock, driven by investments in its forest resources since the mid-2000s.

In terms of origin, FDI stocks in the region are also concentrated in few source countries. The Netherlands and France are the largest investors in the region, jointly accounting for 37% of the region's FDI stock in 2021, while the EU as a whole account for 43% (Figure 1.3). The United States, Canada and the UK jointly hold 18% of the stock of West Africa's FDI stocks, while China accounts for 16%, closely followed by Mauritius and South Africa which together account for 14%. The concentration of investments from the major source economies varies across different markets. The EU as well as the United States, Canada and the United Kingdom held about 65% of their ECOWAS FDI stocks in Nigeria. China, on the other hand, held only about 17% of its ECOWAS FDI stocks in Nigeria while holding 48% in Liberia.

Figure 1.2. FDI stocks are concentrated in Nigeria, Ghana, Côte d'Ivoire and Liberia

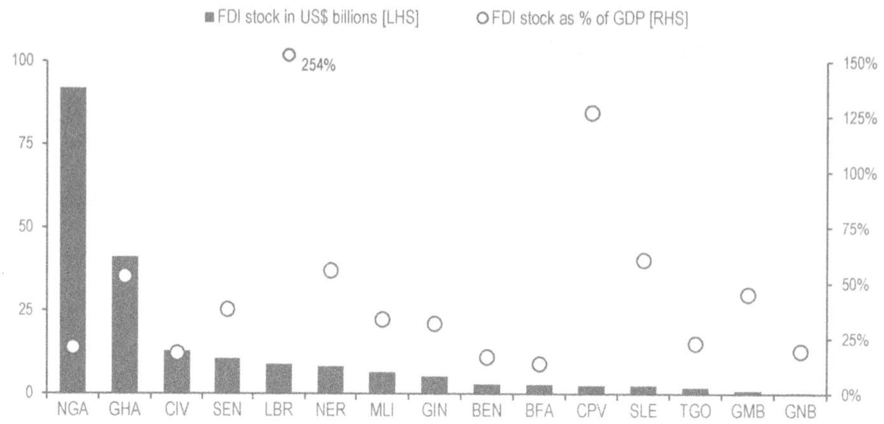

Source: OECD based on UNCTAD (2023[7]) World Bank (2023[8]).

Figure 1.3. The EU represents the largest source of FDI in the ECOWAS region

FDI stock by source and host economy in 2021

Note: The figure is constructed using outward FDI stocks reported by selected source economies in ECOWAS countries in 2021.
Source: OECD based on IMF CDIS (2022[9]).

A core motivation behind efforts to attract FDI is the hope of creating jobs. Greenfield FDI projects in the ECOWAS region created on average three jobs per million USD invested, in line with the world average (Figure 1.4, Panel A). Countries with abundant fossil fuel or metal resources, like Nigeria and Ghana, or low-income countries, like Benin, tend to attract a considerable share of their greenfield FDI in mining and electricity with a relatively few direct jobs created (Figure 1.4, Panel B). Burkina Faso, Guinea-Bissau, and Sierra Leone attracted FDI projects in relatively more labour-intensive service activities, such as customer contact centres, and show above average job creation per million US$ invested.

Figure 1.4. Job intensity of FDI depends on economic structure and stage of development

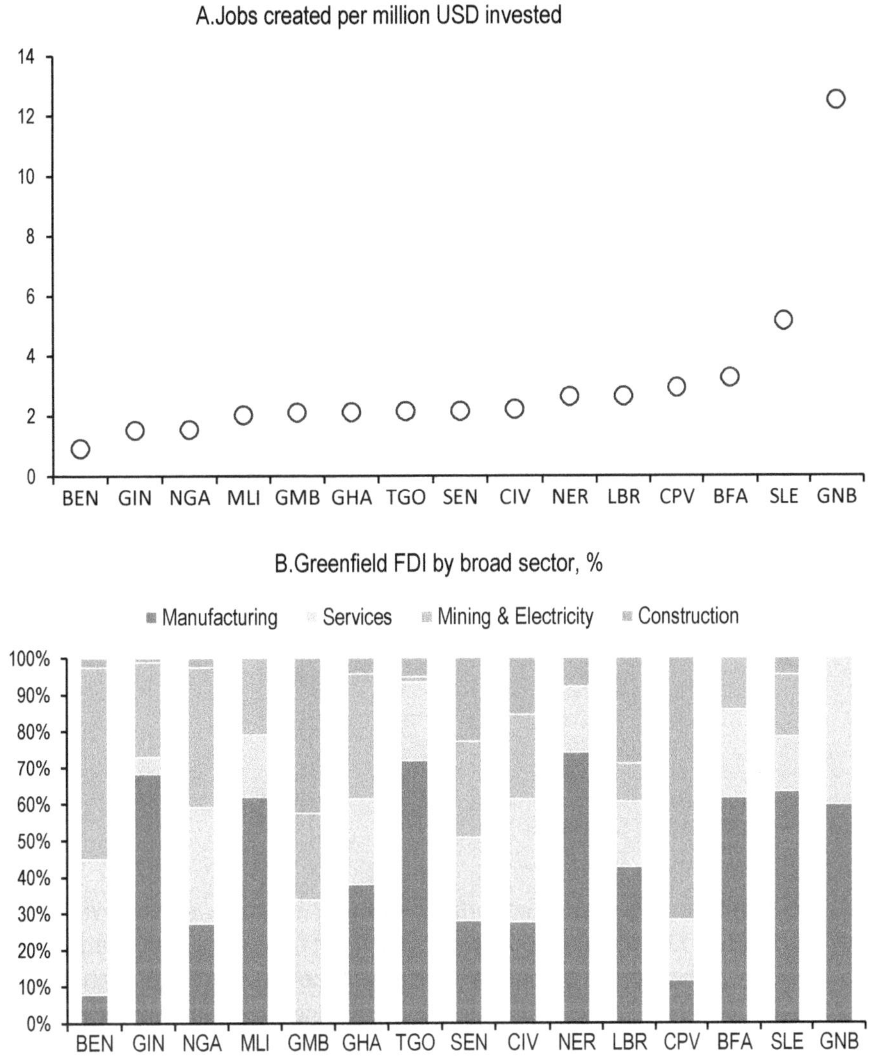

Note: This figure shows the number of direct jobs (Panel A) created by all opened and announced greenfield FDI projects between 2011 and 2022q2 as well as the sectoral split of these FDI flows (Panel B).
Source: OECD based on Financial Times fDi Markets (2023[6]).

Beyond capital and jobs, FDI has the potential to contribute to sustainable development, for instance by introducing new knowledge and technologies. Across ECOWAS members, a significantly larger share of foreign companies claimed to have introduced a new product or service compared to their domestic competitors (Figure 1.5, Panel A). This pattern suggests a greater innovation capacity of foreign firms and thus offers the opportunity of knowledge and technology spillovers to domestic firms. Moreover, by providing more training opportunities for their employees, foreign firms disproportionately contribute to on-the-job skill development within the ECOWAS region, suggesting that FDI plays an important role in raising living standards (Figure 1.5, Panel B). In most ECOWAS countries, foreign firms also employ higher shares of women in their workforce while the share of women in top management positions tends to be higher in domestic companies (Figure 1.5, Panel C-D). The role of FDI in the improvement of gender equality in working life is thus not clear cut as, on the one hand, foreign firms create more employment opportunities for women, whereas, on the other hand, foreign firms do not necessarily offer better career advancement opportunities.

Figure 1.5. FDI is an important driver of productivity and innovation

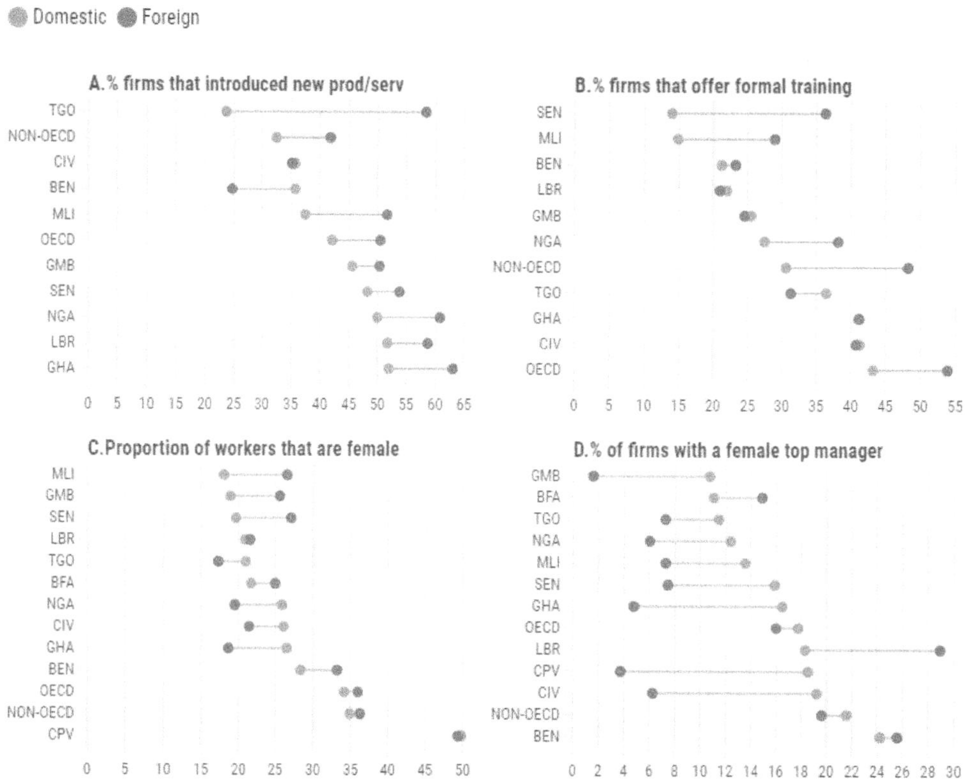

Source: OECD based on World Bank Enterprise Surveys (2023[10]).

FDI in renewables has significantly gained in importance within the energy sector. While FDI in renewables accounted for only 1% of total FDI between 2003 and 2012, it not only increased in absolute terms between 2013 and 2022 but also in proportion to investments in fossil fuels (Figure 1.6, Panel A). Comparing FDI in renewables between 2003 and 2012 to FDI between 2013 and 2022, investments in renewables have increased more than eightfold and accounted for about 10% of total FDI and almost one third of total energy FDI. Although at a lower scale in absolute terms, the proportion of investments in renewables in the ECOWAS region corresponds to the proportion of renewables in other African regions such as SADC. For many ECOWAS countries, FDI in fossil fuels dominate investments in the energy sector while investments in renewable energies only make up a small part (Figure 1.6, Panel B). Although large economies such as Nigeria, or Ghana attract FDI mostly in fossil fuels, they have also received the majority of FDI in renewables within ECOWAS.

Figure 1.6. FDI in renewables has gained in importance in recent years

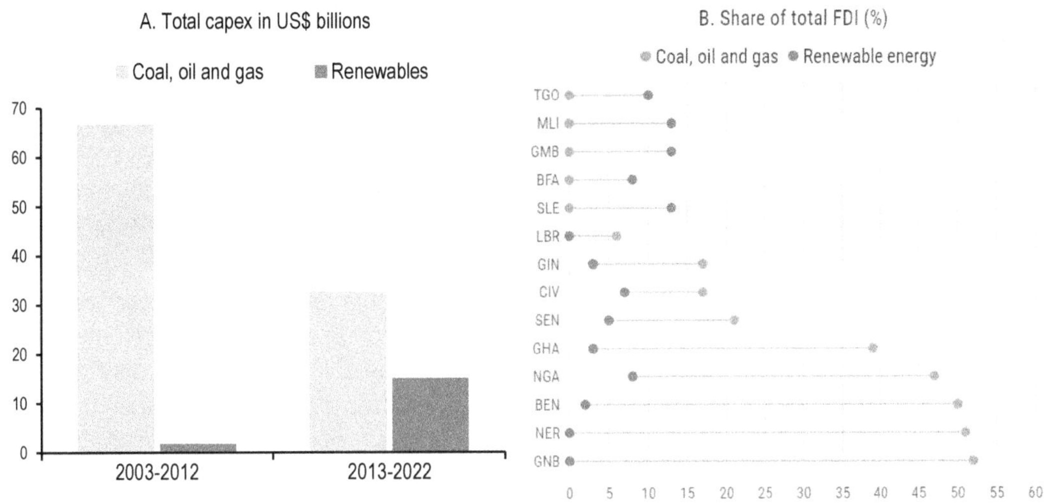

Note: Figure B is calculated using greenfield FDI flows accumulated over 2003-2022.
Source: OECD based on Financial Times (2023[6]) FDI Markets Database.

Key messages and considerations

Sustainable investment has been defined as "commercially viable investment that makes a maximum contribution to the economic, social and environmental development of host countries and takes place in the framework of fair governance mechanisms" (Sauvant and Mann, 2017[11]). A broader definition would consider that sustainable investment should contribute towards achieving the Sustainable Development Goals (SDGs). While an investment project can contribute to several SDGs, trade-offs might also arise when an investment moves the host country closer to some SDGs but farther away from others.

As mentioned at the beginning of this report, the challenge for governments is not just to attract foreign investors at a time of diminishing global FDI flows, but also to ensure that the investment confers sustainable benefits on the host economy. Attracting investment and reaping the maximum benefit in terms of sustainability depend first and foremost on the overall policy framework in which investment occurs. Policymakers need to maintain a sound, transparent and open investment climate, and adopt policies that ensure the benefits of FDI are maximised and their potential harm on the local economy, society and environment are minimised. Furthermore, targeted promotion tools and measures to enable responsible business conduct (RBC) are equally important for a sustainable investment framework. This requires whole-of-government efforts, evidence-based policy-making and meaningful stakeholder consultations.

This report looks primarily at what host governments can do to attract sustainable investment and promote the benefits of investment for social and environmental objectives, including how to facilitate and enable RBC. It provides an analysis to support the ECOWAS Vision 2050, to make ECOWAS a preferred destination for national and foreign investment that is reinforced by effective governance that promotes sustainable and inclusive regional economic development. It is based on the OECD tools, including the Policy Framework for Investment and the FDI Qualities Policy Toolkit and Indicators. Key messages and main considerations that emerge from different chapters are summarised below.

Designing investment frameworks and strategies to promote sustainable investment

- *Increase coherence between national legislation and regional and continental treaties.* The analysis suggests that national investment laws do not yet fully reflect innovations at a regional or continental level, although newer investment laws seem to be closer to regional practice.

Furthermore, there is still considerable diversity in individual laws across the ECOWAS region. Greater coherence in approaches within and across regions in Africa at all levels could contribute to improved clarity and predictability for both governments and investors, although sufficient room should be left for further experimentation at national level.

- *Consider further integrating SDG considerations into investment promotion strategies of ECOWAS Member States.* IPAs in the region should increase focus on attracting FDI that contributes to the SDGs, including by going beyond promoting FDI in renewable energy and integrating other sustainable development sectors and activities. IPAs should consider prioritising investors with good sustainability track-records.
- *Further develop IPAs' value propositions for sustainable investment opportunities*. Several agencies in the region put a particular emphasis on promoting sustainable investment, especially through the promotion of specific sectors such as renewable energy. But only a few provide detailed information on investment opportunities in these sectors and related incentives and legal background. IPAs in the region should enhance their value propositions for sustainable investment opportunities by providing prospective investors with detailed and comprehensive legal and industry information, potentially also bankable projects, and improving their marketing.
- *Put in place adequate key performance indicators (KPIs) to ensure effective prioritisation and sound monitoring and evaluation (M&E) by IPAs*. While it is key to prioritise certain investments over others to respond to sustainability objectives, it is equally important to understand and track their contribution to the desired outcomes. Integrating sustainability indicators in IPA M&E systems is necessary to measure the results of the agency and the effective contribution of companies assisted by the IPA to sustainable development, including the decarbonisation of the economy. ECOWAS IPAs should also ensure that the KPIs used to select priority investments and measure their outcomes are aligned with national development objectives and the agencies' overarching investment promotion priorities. Consider diversifying them to reflect all areas of the SDGs and include sustainable and inclusiveness considerations (e.g. low-carbon transition, gender equality, regional development).
- *Use the SDGs to guide investment facilitation and aftercare services of IPAs to existing investors looking to expand or reinvest.* IPAs should not only focus on promoting sustainable investment through new investments, but also use the SDGs to guide them in the way they deliver investment facilitation and aftercare services to existing investors who wish to expand or reinvest. IPAs in ECOWAS could, for example, consider focusing aftercare activities on those investors with the highest sustainability impacts. They could also take advantage of these services to better promote responsible business conduct within the existing business community and encourage investors to comply with sustainability-related laws more systematically, as well as to embrace responsible practices in their business operations.

Assessing use and design of investment incentives

- *Assess whether investment tax incentives are aligned with investment promotion strategies and SDGs, and consider whether they are the best policy instrument to achieve these goals*. Incentives are not effective as a replacement for other policies to improve the investment climate, including efficient tax administration, quality infrastructure, open and transparent regulatory framework, and good governance. Tax incentives are not always effective to attract investors, while tax revenues are crucial for delivering public goods and services, including those that affect the investment climate. Economic, social and environmental goals might be better supported by other policies, and tax incentives should be used in complement with wider development strategies.
- *Ensure that incentives are designed to generate investments and related outcomes that would not materialise otherwise*. CIT holidays account for more than a third of all incentives offered in the region, and are in some cases permanent, are potentially very costly in terms of foregone revenues.

By eliminating taxes on profit, these incentives heavily favour firms with high profits, which may have invested also in the absence of the incentive. This risk particularly high for tax holidays for extractive activities. Governments should consider phasing out costly profit-based incentives and introducing more targeted types of incentives, that reduce the cost of specific activities that can improve social and environmental outcomes. Improving incentive design, by promoting desired outcomes through tax relief on qualifying expenditure, can help limit redundancies and encourage positive spillovers.

- *Improve monitoring and evaluation of the costs, benefits and uptake of tax incentives*. Better understanding whether incentives contribute to policy goals, and at what costs, requires monitoring and evaluation. Some countries in ECOWAS have started to report on tax expenditure, and several have put in place dedicated teams to conduct fiscal evaluation. However, most countries face administrative, fiscal, data and human resource constraints in administering, monitoring and evaluating incentives. The ECOWAS Commission could play an important role in advocating for improved monitoring and evaluation, as well as transparency and good governance in incentive policies.

Promoting investment for green growth

- *Strengthen NDC targets and develop long-term low-emission development strategies.* Collectively ECOWAS NDCs are not yet aligned with the objectives of the Paris Agreement. Three countries have committed to achieving net-zero GHG emissions by 2050, and another three have submitted long-term strategy documents in addition to their NDCs. Ambitious long-term strategies are vital since current near-term NDCs are only sufficient to limit warming to 2.7-3.7°C. Moreover, long-term strategies provide a pathway to a whole-of-society transformation and a vital link between shorter-term NDCs and the long-term objectives of the Paris Agreement. Given the 30-year time horizon, these strategies offer many other benefits, including guiding countries to avoid costly investments in high-emissions technologies, supporting just and equitable transitions, promoting technological innovation, planning for new sustainable infrastructure in light of future climate risks, and sending early and predictable signals to investors about envisaged long-term societal changes.
- *Use ECOWAS as a platform to promote strategic environmental assessments (SEA) and transboundary environmental impact assessment (EIA).* West African countries made great strides in formalising EIA into their legal frameworks, with most providing for the three critical procedural rights of access to information, public participation, and access to remedies. However, only and four countries in the region have established frameworks for SEAs to examine the environmental and social impact of proposed plans, policies and programmes. Moreover, only two countries have developed a legal framework for application of EIA principles to the assessment of the transboundary impacts of investment, including consultation of the authorities of affected countries. Recognition of transboundary SEA and EIA at the ECOWAS level could encourage other ECOWAS governments to adopt these tools in their national EIA systems.
- *Consider scaling down or phasing out investment incentives for non-green activities.* Seven ECOWAS countries offer corporate income tax holidays to promote investments in coal, oil and gas, and two of these countries offer similar incentives for renewable energy generation. The length of these tax holidays ranges from four years to permanent exemptions and therefore very costly in terms of foregone revenue, while also reducing the ultimate effectiveness of efforts to promote clean energy investment. These countries would benefit from classifying green and nongreen activities in targeted sectors using emerging taxonomies and scaling down or phasing out investment incentives for non-green activities.
- *Consider developing frameworks for voluntary disclosure of environmental and climate impacts.* Frameworks for climate-related disclosure help to reveal how companies are preparing for a lower-carbon economy and support investors to better assess financial exposure to climate-related risks.

To date, climate-related reporting is very limited in West Africa, with only Ghana having developed Sustainable Banking Principles to underpin effective Environmental and Social Risk Management policy frameworks for banks, including reporting requirements for five sectors that are critically sensitive to the environmental and social standards. As of 2020, 24 commercial banks in Ghana agreed to measure and report their progress in implementing the principles. Other countries in the region could follow suit and develop similar frameworks for environmental and climate-related disclosure.

Promoting and enabling responsible business conduct

- *Raise awareness about the relevance and key elements of RBC.* The general awareness about RBC including international standards and due diligence expectations has increased but remains limited in the region. ECOWAS and its Member States could strategically raise awareness and foster the understanding about the relevance of RBC in relation to trade and investment. This could involve learning activities and workshops on international RBC instruments and risk-based due diligence.
- *Create an enabling environment to implement and enforce policies promoting RBC.* ECOWAS Member States have set out concrete policies to promote RBC, as laid out in the ECOWAS Investment Code and in national policies, particularly in the minerals and agricultural sector. Uptake and concrete action to implement these has so far been unclear. National governments could lead the way by developing and implementing National Action Plans on RBC as well as sector or issue-specific reforms.
- *Ensure policy coherence and harmonisation on RBC in line with international standards.* ECOWAS represents a policy forum to foster coherence and harmonisation of RBC policies in line with the most important international RBC standards, such as the OECD MNE Guidelines and the OECD due diligence guidance. ECOWAS could take the next step to create strong alignment and coordination of policies on RBC among Member States to ensure a common approach and level-playing field at the regional level.
- *Build the capacity of companies to carry out due diligence.* ECOWAS and its Member States could promote the use of the OECD due diligence framework by enterprises in ECOWAS and actively support the uptake of due diligence by companies, investors, and other stakeholders.

References

ECOWAS (2018), *ECOWAS Common Investment Code*, https://wacomp.projects.ecowas.int/wp-content/uploads/2020/03/ECOWAS-COMMON-INVESTMENT-CODEENGLISH.pdf. [2]

ECOWAS (2018), *ECOWAS Investment Policy*, https://wacomp.projects.ecowas.int/wp-content/uploads/2020/03/ECOWAS-INVESTMENT-POLICY-ENGLISH.pdf. [1]

ECOWAS (2008), *Supplementary Act A/SA.3/12/08 Adopting Community Rules on Investment and the Modalities for their Implementation with ECOWAS*, https://ecowas.int/. [3]

Financial Times (2023), *FDI Markets: the in-depth crossborder investment monitor from the Financial Times*, https://www.fdimarkets.com/. [6]

IMF (2023), *Balance of Payments and International Investment Positions*, https://data.imf.org/BOP. [5]

IMF (2022), *Coordinated Direct Investment Survey (CDIS)*, https://data.imf.org/. [9]

Sauvant, K. and H. Mann (2017), *Towards an Indicative List of FDI Sustainability Characteristics*, https://ssrn.com/abstract=3055961. [11]

UNCTAD (2023), *FDI/MNE Database*, http://www.unctad.org/fdistatistics. [7]

World Bank (2023), *Nigeria Overview: Development news, research, data | World Bank*, https://www.worldbank.org/en/country/nigeria/overview (accessed on 2 February 2023). [4]

World Bank (2023), *World Bank Enterprise Surveys*, https://www.enterprisesurveys.org/en/data. [10]

World Bank (2023), *World Development Indicators*, https://databank.worldbank.org/. [8]

2 Rebalancing and aligning investment policy for sustainable development

This chapter undertakes a baseline comparative analysis of the legal framework governing investment at the continental, regional and national levels in ECOWAS. The analysis focuses on how governments in ECOWAS are incorporating sustainability dimensions into their national treaties and domestic investment laws, as well as on the coherence between action at the national, regional and international levels.

Investment policymaking today is placing greater emphasis on sustainable outcomes as part of a broader shift away from investment for its own sake and towards a more nuanced appraisal of its potential impact. As such, this new approach is generally to be welcomed, but many of the innovations are relatively recent. It is too soon to assess which provisions will have a lasting positive impact on sustainable development. The impact on attractiveness for foreign and domestic investment also remains unclear.

What is clear is that sustainable development requires both substantial investment and good regulation. The legal framework for investment comprises two levels: (i) a domestic regime involving many laws regulating market activities, often supplemented in Africa by an investment law; and (ii) international treaties that offer additional provisions and protections applicable to covered foreign investors. The international regime is in turn divided into bilateral, regional, and plurilateral approaches, including investment treaties as well as free trade agreements (FTAs) with an investment chapter.

At the international level, the new approach to sustainability can encompass several facets, from hortatory clauses in the Preamble or articles, to limitations on the scope of protections, to investor obligations. To date, concrete impact in preserving policy space has been difficult to demonstrate (OECD, 2022[1]).

A key factor in effectiveness of sustainability efforts may be regional standard-setting coupled with effective and aligned action at the domestic level. The development of regional approaches can allow a full debate with greater resources. National implementation aligned with regional approaches can increase visibility and coherence of the measures.

In Africa, sustainability dimensions are likely to become even more important once the African Continental Free Trade Area (AfCFTA) Investment Protocol is finalised. These developments will raise the issue of alignment between regional and national action. Comparing regional and national approaches to sustainable development is challenging. This chapter engages in an initial analysis to compare innovations at the regional and continental level with the approaches embodied in national investment-related legislation within ECOWAS. The analysis focuses on how governments in ECOWAS are incorporating sustainability dimensions into their national treaties and domestic investment laws, as well as on the coherence between action at the national and regional/international levels.

The analysis below suggests that national investment laws do not yet fully reflect innovations at a regional or continental level, although newer investment laws seem to be closer to regional practice. Furthermore, there is still considerable diversity in individual laws across the ECOWAS region. Greater coherence in approaches within and across regions in Africa at all levels could contribute to improved clarity and predictability for both governments and investors, although sufficient room should be left for further experimentation at national level.

The international regime for investment protection is under increasing strain

More than 2,500 bilateral investment treaties (BITs) and multilateral agreements with an investment chapter or provisions are in force today. Traditionally, these agreements focused on the protection of investors and investments at the post-establishment phase and had as their main goal to foster foreign investments, including by providing more legal certainty and reducing unwarranted risks for foreign investors. These international investment agreements (IIAs) constitute an important part of a country's investment framework as they offer protections and guarantees that often go beyond what is included in domestic investment laws.

IIAs typically offer covered investors substantive and procedural protection. Classic substantive standards of protection include, for instance, the protection against unlawful expropriation and against discrimination, whether between foreign and domestic investors or among foreign investors, through the National Treatment (NT) and Most-Favoured Nation (MFN) provisions. They also often cover the guarantee of fair and equitable (FET) treatment and of full protection and security (FPS), which are sometimes equated with the international minimum standard of treatment of aliens under customary international law. Lastly, they also provide a guarantee for the free transfer of funds and profits in and out of host states. From a procedural point of view, most IIAs provide for an investor-state dispute settlement (ISDS) mechanism, which allows investors to bring claims against the state in which they invested before international arbitral tribunals for an alleged breach of the IIA.

States are currently reconsidering the role, purpose and content of investment treaties, particularly the earlier generation treaties, for several reasons. Firstly, investor-state arbitration cases have risen exponentially in the past decade, including cases involving public policy or regulatory measures, with the added risk of a regulatory chill to avoid the possibility of future disputes. Secondly, academic studies have reached inconclusive results with regard to whether the treaties increase inflows of investment. Thirdly, societal demands are mounting that international investment should contribute positively to sustainable development. It is increasingly recognised that while FDI can play a crucial role in making progress toward all SDGs, particularly in advancing decarbonisation, increasing innovation, creating quality jobs, developing human capital and promoting gender equality, the effects of FDI are not always positive and impacts can differ across areas of sustainable development.

Partly as a result, some countries such as India, Indonesia and South Africa have terminated their treaties. Many other governments have worked to improve the functioning and perceived fairness of treaties. The United Nations Commission on International Trade Law (UNCITRAL) is currently working on a comprehensive reform of the investor-state dispute settlement (ISDS) system. The OECD is also embarked on a work programme on the Future of Investment Treaties, with one track addressing investment treaties and climate change, and the other considering updating older treaties to conform to approaches widely used in recent treaties.

Treaty innovations at regional and continental level in Africa

Different countries and regions have adopted different strategies for reform, and Africa has in many ways been at the forefront of innovative approaches. These can be seen in the non-binding Pan-African Investment Code, and likely in the Investment Protocol as part of the AfCFTA, once it is completed, as well as regional approaches in the Southern African Development Community (SADC), Economic Community of West African States (ECOWAS) and elsewhere. They place much greater emphasis on achieving sustainable development outcomes from treaties, as explained below.

An increasing number of states and regional organisations, including African states and Regional Economic Communities, incorporate sustainable development considerations in their new investment agreements or model agreements and adopt innovative provisions on various policy issues. The analysis of some investment instruments adopted in Africa at the continental and regional levels reveals the states' desire to: (i) attract and protect investments that foster sustainable development; (ii) preserve their regulatory policy space, including on sustainable development-related policy issues, by better delineating and limiting some of the core standards of protection; (iii) achieve a better balance between the investors' and states' rights and obligations, including on sustainable development-related matters; (iv) make commitments on sustainable development-related issues; and (v) redesign the ISDS system.

This section reviews developments in the following regional and continental approaches:

- The SADC Finance and Investment Protocol, particularly Annex 1 on co-operation on investment (SADC FIP, signed 2006, entered into force 2010 and as revised as per the Agreement Amending Annex 1 signed in 2017);
- The SADC Model BIT (2012, a 2017 version is not available);
- The ECOWAS Supplementary Act Adopting Community Rules on Investment and the Modalities for their Implementation (ECOWAS SA, signed 2008, in force 2009);

- The ECOWAS Common Investment Code (ECOWIC, adopted in 2018);
- The draft Pan-African Investment Code (PAIC, 2016).

Language in the Preamble and in separate articles

The preambles of the SADC Model BIT and the ECOWIC provide that the parties to these instruments are "seeking to promote, encourage and increase investment opportunities that enhance sustainable development within the territories of the State Parties". The preambles also often expressly recognise the key role of investment or the private sector in achieving various sustainable development objectives, such as the reduction of poverty, the increase of productive capacity or the furtherance of human rights and human development. All of the instruments repeat the sustainable development objective in a separate article. The SADC Model BIT, ECOWIC and PAIC set out the characteristics that an investment must have to be protected (based on the Salini test in the ICSID jurisprudence), including the "significant contribution to the host State's economic development" (e.g. art. 4(4) of the PAIC).

All instruments set out in their definition of "investment" several exclusions, particularly for "portfolio investments" and certain "investments of a speculative nature". This underlines the states' desire to attract long-term or more substantial investments which have a better chance to make a positive contribution to sustainable development. Some instruments, such as the ECOWIC and PAIC, also exclude from their coverage "investments in any sector sensitive to its development or which would have an adverse impact on its economy" (art. 1(h) and art. 4(4) respectively).

Better delineation of substantive standards of protection, affirmation of the state's right to regulate and general exclusions to seek to preserve policy space on key sustainable development-related matters

The investment instruments clarify, limit and sometimes delete certain substantive standards, mainly to preserve policy space. The most recent instruments all contain detailed provisions on non-discrimination (which usually cover the National Treatment (NT) and Most-Favoured Nation (MFN) principles, apart from the SADC instruments which only cover the former) and on the protection against expropriation. They set out numerous limitations and exceptions to these standards, some of which are particularly relevant from a sustainable development point of view. For instance, nearly all the instruments list examples of elements that should be considered when assessing whether investors or investments are in "like circumstances" for the purpose of NT or MFN principles and refer to the effect on the environment. Some also authorise the adoption of measures that derogate from the NT and/or MFN principles, including regulatory measures designed and applied to protect or enhance legitimate public welfare objectives, such as public health, safety and the environment (ECOWIC, art. 7; and PAIC, art. 8 and 10 - provided they are not arbitrary). Certain instruments also exclude from the scope of MFN treatment dispute settlement procedures and/or substantive obligations of other treaties (e.g. ECOWAS SA, art, 6(1) or PAIC, art. 7(4)) which preclude investors from invoking broader provisions than those contained in these instruments. Lastly, some instruments provide that measures designed and applied to protect or enhance legitimate public welfare objectives, such as public health, safety and the environment, do not constitute indirect expropriation (the PAIC adds that the measure must be non-discriminatory but not the revised version of Annex 1 of the SADC PFI, while the SADC Model BIT leaves a choice).

The most recent instruments do not include an FET provision. The initial version of Annex 1 to the ECOWAS SA contains the FET standard but qualifies it by reference to customary international law. Some instruments also list a series of obligations relating to procedural fairness which, if breached, could constitute a breach of this standard (ECOWAS SA, art. 19). The SADC Model BIT advocates for an alternative and more restrictive option, "fair administrative treatment", which protects, inter alia, against denial of justice, un-remedied and egregious violations of due process, targeted discrimination on manifestly unjustified grounds and manifestly abusive treatment.

The instruments also aim at preserving the state's right to regulate on sustainable development-related issues by affirming this right in the agreement and by providing general exceptions. All instruments except the ECOWAS ones refer to the right to regulate and/or to the balance of rights and obligations between investors and states in their preamble. The SADC instruments also contain a separate provision affirming, inter alia, the right to take regulatory or other measures to ensure that "development in their territory is consistent with the goals and principles of sustainable development, and with other legitimate social and economic policy objectives" (art. 20). All instruments except the Annex 1 of the SADC PFI (both versions) also set out general exceptions for various measures including, inter alia, those aimed at protecting human, animal or plant life and the environment or at promoting the achievement of equality in their territory or designed to protect or advance persons or categories of persons disadvantaged by long term historic discrimination (usually provided these are applied in a non-arbitrary and non-discriminatory manner). Certain instruments also authorise the state to take non-discriminatory measures to comply with its international obligations under other treaties, which could include, for instance, measures aimed at achieving the commitment of the Paris agreements or other conventions or standards that promote sustainable development (SADC Model BIT, art. 6, revised version of Annex 1 of the SADC PFI, art. 5).

Introduction of a broad range of investor obligations and mechanisms to address breaches

All instruments incorporate a broad range of obligations for investors, many of which relate to sustainable development (except for both versions of Annex 1 of the SADC PFI). The PAIC and the ECOWIC are the most comprehensive in this respect. All instruments set out a general obligation to comply with domestic laws and regulations for investors and/or their investments. Most (except both versions of Annex 1 of the SADC PFI) also incorporate more specific pre- and post-establishment obligations for investors on a wide range of topics, including the environment, labour practices and standards, human rights, corruption or corporate social responsibility (CSR).

Investors are required to conduct environmental and sometimes social impact assessment (ECOWAS SA, art. 12, ECOWIC, art. 27 and PAIC, art. 37) or to comply with the assessment screening criteria and processes applicable to the proposed investment, as required by the laws of the host state or home state or international standards, whichever is the most rigorous (SADC Model BIT, art. 13, which requires considering impacts on human rights). Many instruments specify that the precautionary principle should be applied when conducting such assessments and to decisions taken in relation to a proposed investment. Investors are also required to comply with domestic environmental laws and multilateral agreements (ECOWIC, art. 27), protect the environment in performing their activities (PAIC, art. 37), repair any damages caused (PAIC, art. 37; ECOWIC, art. 27), maintain an environmental management system (SADC Model BIT, art. 14) or use environmentally sound management practices (ECOWIC, art. 29).

All instruments (except both versions of Annex 1 of the SADC PFI) provide that investors shall not engage in corrupt practices (as a main author or as an accomplice) before or after the establishment of the investment. Many also impose obligations related to human rights (such as the obligation to uphold, support and respect such rights, not to undertake any act that would breach these rights or be an accomplice to such acts) and labour, such as the obligation to act in accordance with or apply the standards stipulated in the 1998 ILO Declaration (the SADC Model BIT and ECOWAS SA) or, more generally, to comply with international conventions on labour issues (the PAIC). Some instruments include specific obligations concerning CSR but also hortatory clauses. The ECOWIC provides that investors "shall endeavour to promote and engage in CSR in accordance with international best practices" (art. 34).

The ECOWIC and PAIC also include certain obligations but also hortatory clauses concerning the transfer and diffusion of technology (including horizontal obligations, i.e. applicable to the state as well). The ECOWIC imposes an obligation on investors "to adopt, where practicable in the course of their business activities, practices that permit the transfer and rapid diffusion of technologies" and "to diffuse technology and upgrades as well as improvements thereof through various mechanisms such as the demonstration and competition effects, the movement of labour from foreign affiliates to local firms and through the creation of linkages between foreign and local companies and their customers" (art. 47 and 48; the PAIC uses hortatory language for the first obligation).

The enforceability for such obligations can vary and is not always clear. The ECOWAS SA is the most comprehensive on this topic while both versions of Annex 1 of the SADC PFI and the ECOWIC remain silent. Various consequences are foreseen under different treaties. For instance, several instruments (i) provide that the tribunal or competent adjudicatory body shall consider whether an alleged breach of obligations raised by the host state, if proven, is materially relevant to the issues before it, and if so, what mitigating or off-setting effects this may have on the merits of a claim or on the damages awarded (if any); and (ii) authorise to bring counterclaims against the investor (SADC Model BIT, art. 19(1) and (2); ECOWAS SA, art. 18(2), (4) and (5) and PAIC, art. 43(1) and (2)). Some of these instruments authorise the home or host state (or other actors) to initiate proceedings before a tribunal established under the instrument or to initiate civil action before the domestic courts for the breach of certain or all obligations (ECOWAS SA, art. 18(3) and SADC Model BIT art. 19(3) and (4)).

The breaches of corruption-related obligations often have separate consequences. The ECOWAS SA provides that a breach of such obligations, if established by a court, can prevent an investor from initiating dispute settlement procedures under this instrument (art. 18(1)). The SADC Model BIT considers that a breach of the article on corruption is "deemed to constitute a breach of the domestic law of the Host State concerning the establishment and operation of an investment" and therefore constitutes a breach of the treaty (art. 10(3) and 17(4) respectively). Many instruments also require the state parties to prosecute, and where convicted, penalise such acts of corruption.

Lastly, certain instruments further provide that investors can be subject to civil actions before the domestic courts of their home state or the host state for acts and decisions made in relation to their investment when such acts and decisions have led to "significant damage, personal injuries or loss of life" in the host state (ECOWAS SA, art. 17; see also SADC Model BIT, art. 17 which also includes "omissions" and does not require that such acts, decisions or omissions are made in relation to investment). The SADC Model BIT further adds that "home states shall ensure that their legal systems and rules allow for, or do not prevent or unduly restrict such actions" (see also, ECOWAS SA, art. 29).

State commitments and obligations concerning key sustainable development matters

All instruments contain obligations and commitments for the state parties concerning key sustainable development matters, including on the environment, labour, human rights and corruption. Like for the investors' obligations, both versions of Annex 1 of the SADC PFI are relatively succinct on this issue. By contrast, the ECOWIC is particularly detailed and sets out a broad range of commitments and obligations for the member states.

All instruments explicitly require the state parties not to lower certain standards. Most provide that the states recognise that "it is inappropriate" to encourage investment by relaxing labour, health, safety or environmental measures or some subset of these measures (both versions of Annex 1 of the SADC PFI, art. 13 and 11, ECOWAS SA, art. 20) or "domestic environmental and labour legislation" (SADC Model BIT). The ECOWIC goes further by providing that member states recognise that "it is unlawful" "to encourage investment by relaxing national health, safety or environmental measures" and by "reducing the protection afforded in their respective environmental laws" (art 21-22). Concerning labour, the ECOWIC uses less stringent language and provides that member states recognise that "it is inappropriate to encourage investment by relaxing domestic labour legislation" (art. 30). As a consequence, states parties commit not to waive or derogate from these measures and laws as an encouragement for investment. The original and revised versions of Annex 1 of the SADC PFI add that member states "agree not to waive or other derogate from international treaties they have ratified" as an encouragement for investment (art. 13

and 11). It is worth noting that the SADC Model BIT and ECOWIC provide for a consultation mechanism in case a member state breaches this obligation (art. 22(2) and. 21(4) respectively).

Many instruments include declarations and commitments by the state parties concerning their environmental, labour and human rights rules and standards. In certain instruments, the states, for instance, recognise the importance of multilateral agreements to which they are a party (ECOWIC, art. 23 for environmental agreements) or commit to implement them (ECOWIC, art. 23). Concerning domestic laws and regulations, most instruments provide that state parties shall (or "shall strive to") ensure that they provide for high levels of environmental, labour and/or human rights protection (in some cases adding that international standards or treaties shall be taken into account (ECOWAS SA, art. 21(2)) and shall strive to continue to improve those laws and regulations. Certain instruments add that they shall also ensure their laws and regulation are consistent with international labour standards and/or international human rights agreements (ECOWAS SA, art. 21).

Many of the instruments also impose obligations on the states concerning the fight against corruption (ECOWIC, chapter 9, SADC Model BIT, art. 10 and ECOWAS SA, art. 30). Noticeably, the ECOWIC contains an obligation to ratify or adhere to the UN Convention against Corruption (art. 35(4)). Certain instruments, particularly the PAIC but more importantly the ECOWIC, impose other obligations on the states e.g. concerning the protection of the environment. The PAIC provides that the states shall undertake environmental impact assessments and that, with the investors, they should take all practical steps to promote, facilitate and finance the transfer of or access to environmentally sound technology and know-how (art. 30 and 37). In the ECOWIC, the member states also recognise the importance of public participation and regional cooperation on this important issue (art. 26(1)).

The instruments include various other commitments and obligations for the states which could also affect sustainable development, concerning, for instance, investment promotion and facilitation (including through investment promotion agencies and through the home state's assistance), the transparency and accessibility of investment legal framework, the cooperation on investment related issues or the protection of fair competition or intellectual property rights.

Alternatives and additions to the traditional ISDS mechanism

Faced with growing criticism of the ISDS mechanism, the instruments adopt different innovative approaches: ISDS is either excluded or, if included, is subject to various conditions, such as prior consultations and negotiations, exhaustion of domestic remedies or respect of certain time limits. Many instruments also encourage the use of alternative dispute resolution mechanisms such as mediation before initiating arbitration proceedings. These modifications reduce the risk of potential challenges to non-discriminatory regulatory measures, such as those adopted to achieve sustainable development objectives.

The original version of Annex 1 of the SADC PFI contains an ISDS provision. Under this instrument, investor-state disputes which have not been amicably settled, can be submitted to arbitration but only after exhaustion of local remedies (art. 28). The SADC Model BIT's preferred option is a state-state dispute settlement mechanism, which allows the state parties to bring claims on behalf of the investor subject to the fulfilment of several conditions (exhaustion of local remedies and respect of certain time limits to bring the claim) (art. 28). It sets out an example of an ISDS provision, in case the states decide to negotiate and include such a mechanism in their agreement but sets out numerous conditions (including those mentioned above) (art. 29). The 2016 version of Annex 1 of the SADC PFI deleted the ISDS provision but guarantees investors access to the domestic courts "for redress of their grievance in relation to any matter concerning their investment" (art. 25).

The language used in the ECOWAS SA is not fully clear on whether investor-state arbitration is possible. The ECOWIC provides that disputes between an investor and a member state may be resolved through various means including arbitration. The latter may be conducted at "any established public or private alternative dispute resolution centres or the arbitration division of the ECOWAS Court of Justice" but encourages use of regional and local alternative dispute settlement institutions. The Code adds that when investment contracts between a member state and an investor provide for the use of international mechanisms such as ICSID or UNCITRAL, the parties to such contracts "shall exhaust all local remedies including the ECOWAS Court of Justice or national dispute settlement systems" before resorting to these mechanisms (art. 54).

Recent studies argue that the PAIC "offers a middle ground solution to African States that are either pro-ISDS or anti-ISDS" as it leaves the use of ISDS to the discretion of member states (Mbengue and Schacherer, 2021[2]). The PAIC provides that "member states may, in line with their domestic policies, agree to utilize the [ISDS] mechanism" (art. 42(1)). Disputing parties must first seek resolution through consultations and negotiations, if they fail, the dispute may be resolved through arbitration, subject to the applicable laws of the host state and/or the mutual agreement of the parties and subject to exhaustion of local remedies (art. 43(1(d)). The PAIC also contains a fork-in-the-road provision preventing multiple proceedings (art. 43(2)).

Investment laws of the ECOWAS member states

The introduction of innovative provisions at the regional and continental levels seems to have had some spill-over benefits at domestic regulatory level. While domestic investment laws have a wider scope than IIAs – covering, for instance, the regulation of the admission of investments or the provision of incentives – they may also contain similar features, such as rights and guarantees for investors and investments.

While investment legislation involves many layers of rules and regulations covering different areas, this analysis is limited only to investment laws (and, when easily identifiable, to the accompanying regulations). It does not cover, for instance, general tax laws which may offer additional incentives, nor enterprise laws or commercial codes acts which may impose separate obligations on investors, as well as arbitration laws. This analysis also does not cover sectoral legislation which may regulate investment in specific sectors, nor wider legislation and constitutions which may provide further details on, for instance, the rules for nationalisation and expropriation. Consequently, it is not because a specific element aimed at enhancing sustainable development is absent from the investment law, such as an investor's obligation to protect the environment, that it is not provided for in separate legislation. Investment laws nevertheless often encapsulate a government's overall approach to investment policy and to the potential role of investment in attaining sustainable development objectives.

All ECOWAS member states have an investment law covering both domestic and foreign investments. The great majority of these laws were adopted or amended in the 2010s and 2020s. The most recent laws are in Benin, Burkina Faso, Côte d'Ivoire and Togo and the oldest are those of Nigeria, Senegal and Sierra Leone. The laws described in this section are listed below:

- Benin: *Law on Investment Code* (2020)
- Burkina Faso: *Law on the Investment Code* (2018)
- Cabo Verde: *Investment Law* (2012, amended in 2013)
- Côte d'Ivoire: *Ordonnance on the Investment Code* (2018)
- The Gambia: *Investment and Export Promotion Act* (2015)
- Ghana: *Investment Promotion Center Act* (2013)
- Guinea: *Code of Investment* (2015)
- Liberia: *Investment Act* (2010)
- Mali: *Law on the Investment Code* (2012)
- Niger: *Investment Code* (2014)
- Nigeria: *Investment Promotion Commission Act* (1995, amended in 2004?)

- Senegal: *Investment Code* (2004)
- Sierra Leone: *Investment Law* (2004)
- Togo: *Law on Investment Code* (2019)

The scope of the investment laws varies from one country to another. Some laws such as in Ghana or Nigeria primarily focus on the investment promotion agency while others focus instead on advantages and incentives on offer, together with their eligibility conditions, and set out the rules applicable to special zones, such as in Togo or Benin. But they all contain more or less detailed provisions on the rights and guarantees of investors and investments and, in some instances, impose obligations on them.

The introduction of innovative provisions at the regional and continental level seems to have spilled over, to some extent, to the domestic regulatory level. Some of the most recent laws reveal the state's desire to (i) attract and protect investments that could positively contribute to sustainable development; (ii) provide obligations for investors in investment laws, including on sustainable development-related issues, and mechanisms to sanction the breach of these obligations; and, to a more limited extent, (iii) rethink the investor-state dispute mechanisms. In contrast with the regional and continental investment instruments analysed above, the clarification of the standard of protection clauses and the commitments and obligations on the state concerning sustainable development-related issues are relatively limited in the ECOWAS investment laws.

Sustainability language and sustainable development objectives in the most recent laws

As with regional investment instruments, several of the most recent ECOWAS investment laws contain sustainability language in the article setting out the purpose of the law and, more rarely, in their preamble. Côte d'Ivoire provides that one of the objectives of the law is "to foster sustainable development through productive and socially responsible investments" (art. 3). Liberia, in the preamble, recognises the "urgent need" to revise its former law on investment "to ensure consistency with international best practice as a necessary tool for attracting sustainable domestic and foreign investment". Togo and Benin provide that the objective of their investment laws is to "promote, facilitate and protect sustainable and responsible investment", and both set out more detailed objectives in this respect. For instance, Benin's law aims to encourage the creation and development of activities which, inter alia, promote "the creation of sustainable and decent jobs, the training of national cadres and the emergence of a skilled national workforce", as well as "green industry and environmental protection" (art. 2). Guinea's law aims to establish the legal and institutional framework for private investments to foster certain objectives, many of which relate to sustainable development (including those mentioned for Benin). Burkina Faso refers to promoting "productive investments that contribute to the country's social and economic development (art. 2). Eight ECOWAS member states nevertheless make no reference to sustainability in either the Preamble or in an article setting out the purpose of the law.

Further elements of investment laws relating to sustainable investment are however worth noting:

- Cabo Verde's law provides that the investments shall be subordinated to, inter alia, "the principles and objectives of national economic and environmental policy" and that they "should help" achieve various objectives, including objectives related to sustainable development (art. 3). This language differs from that used at the regional level, depending on whether the benefit of this law could be denied if the investment does not help to achieve or actually impedes these objectives.
- Burkina Faso's law requires prior authorisation of the investor from the Minister of Industry. The application must contain various elements including the impact on the environment and safeguard measures.
- Some laws set out specific advantages and incentives for investments in sectors or activities that positively contribute to sustainable development or deny certain advantages in case of potential adverse impact on sustainable development. Burkina Faso sets out more favourable eligibility

conditions for certain advantages, extends them and provides for additional ones for companies working in various sectors including the renewable energy sector and the protection of the environment (art. 17 and 32; see also the Gambia, Section 41 and Schedule II). Togo provides that the certificate approving the granting of incentives may be denied in case of expected or serious risk of adverse impacts on the environment, public health or national security (art. 23).

- Lastly, while investment laws often exclude certain sectors or activities from their scope and, in some limited instances, list the sectors of activities that are covered, a very limited number of laws expressly exclude or include sectors or activities that could negatively or positively contribute to sustainable development. Niger provides a positive list of activities that are covered by the Code, including the production of renewable energy. The Gambia provides that investment is prohibited in certain fields, including in an enterprise which is detrimental to the natural environment, public health or which contravenes domestic laws (Section 29).

All national investment laws except four (Côte d'Ivoire, the Gambia, Nigeria and Sierra Leone) have a separate provision setting out the principle of non-discrimination post-establishment with very few relevant limitations (from a sustainable development point of view). In Burkina Faso, Niger and Senegal, NT is subject to reciprocity. Benin, Côte d'Ivoire and Guinea, a derogation is made for large and important projects or to promote domestic entrepreneurship. The remaining ECOWAS member states allow for derogations to NT for measures affecting all investors or if specifically provided for under applicable legislation. Thus, while many ECOWAS members allow for some general derogation, the approach is different from that at a regional level which focuses more on the meaning of "like circumstances" and allows for discriminatory measures "in order to achieve national development objectives" (SADC PFI).

Many of the investment laws are very succinct on the protection against expropriation and only two set out exceptions to this principle. Burkina Faso and Togo both provide that the regulatory measures designed and applied to protect public interests such as public health, security or the environment do not constitute an indirect expropriation (art. 8 and 6 respectively; Togo's law specifies that the measure must be non-discriminatory).

Two recent laws contain an FET standard without defining it precisely. Côte d'Ivoire includes an unqualified FET standard providing that, subject to bilateral, regional and multilateral agreements signed by the state, foreign natural and legal persons enjoy FET concerning the rights and obligations related to their investments (art. 25). The FET standard in Burkina Faso's law is qualified but remains relatively vague. It provides that foreign enterprises enjoy FET (and constant security and protection) thereby protecting the investor against any unjustified or discriminatory measures that could impede, in law or in fact, the management, maintenance, usage, benefice or liquidation of their investments (art. 12). No ECOWAS member state includes a reference to "fair and administrative treatment".

In other areas, it is worth noting that national investment laws in ECOWAS are usually more detailed on the guarantee of free transfer of funds and that several set out limitations to this principle. Côte d'Ivoire provides that the state can prevent a transfer of funds through the fair, non-discriminatory and good faith application of its texts concerning, inter alia, the protection of the environment (art. 28).

Incorporation of sustainable development related obligations for investors and mechanisms to sanction a breach of these obligations

Like the regional investment instruments analysed above, a great number of national investment laws impose obligations on investors and their investments (either on all of them or on those benefiting from specific advantages). Certain laws such as in Guinea and Benin contain separate chapters or sections on these obligations and provide a wide range of obligations, while others provide more ad hoc obligations. This practice is intended to strike a balance between guarantees offered to investors and conditions that investors must respect in order to be eligible for these guarantees and for incentives.

A great majority of the investment laws include a general obligation for investors and their investment to comply with domestic legislation and regulations, such as in Benin, Côte d'Ivoire, Guinea, the Gambia, and Niger. Many of these laws also impose pre and/or post-establishment obligations. While some of these obligations concern sustainable development related areas, they are more limited in scope and content than those contained in the regional ECOWAS investment instruments analysed above.

A limited number of investment laws impose pre-establishment obligations, relating mainly to corruption (e.g. art. 25 of Benin's Law provides that "the investor shall refrain from any act of corruption and any act of related offences before, during and after his establishment"; see also art. 26 of Guinea's *Investment Code*) and to the protection of the environment (e.g. Togo's law, art. 20, which requires investors to submit an environmental impact assessment when applying for specific advantages and incentives). Certain laws also sanction the provision of false or misleading statements when applying for specific advantages or incentives, which could be interpreted as a "pre-establishment obligation".

Post-establishment obligations are more frequent (as are post-establishment guarantees). Several laws require investors to comply with specific legislation and regulations including those relating to the environment and labour (e.g. Ghana, art. 34; Niger, art. 15; or Togo, art. 37), and, more rarely, to human rights or CSR (Guinea, art. 21-24; or Côte d'Ivoire, art. 36). Certain laws contain more specific obligations concerning the environment and require the investor to protect the environment by taking all necessary and appropriate measures (the Gambia, Schedule I, Part II) or by resorting to processes and technical equipment that are deemed to be the most suitable by the competent services (Burkina Faso, art. 20). Others impose more specific obligations on labour-related issues, particularly for investors or enterprises benefitting from specific advantages or incentives. Investors are often required to recruit local workers in priority at equal qualifications, to contribute to developing their skills through training and technology transfer, and to promote them (Senegal, art. 25; Mali, art. 28; Togo, art. 37; or Benin, art. 23). Lastly, some of these laws, such as in Côte d'Ivoire (art. 36), oblige the investor to refrain from any acts of corruption or to adopt ethics rules on corruption and internal and external control system for work processes.

Like the regional ECOWAS investment instruments, many of investment laws also contain mechanisms to sanction the potential breach of these obligations in different ways. Several laws provide that a breach of the obligations set out in these laws can lead to the suspension or the withdrawal of the advantages granted and/or of the certificate approving the advantages, to the repayment of the taxes and other fees that were not paid, and/or to a fine (e.g. Benin, art. 25). Côte d'Ivoire provides that the certificate approving the advantages can be withdrawn for a breach of environmental obligations that could have consequences for human and animal health (art. 48). Certain laws, such as in Togo (art. 17), also specify that the investment promotion agency or another competent body should ensure compliance with these obligations.

Limited sustainable development related obligations for states

In contrast with ECOWAS investment instruments, national investment laws do not incorporate states' obligations or commitments on key sustainable development issues such as the protection of the environment, the respect of labour standards and human rights or the fight against corruption. But several ECOWAS member states do make other commitments in these laws which could positively contribute to sustainable development. Some states undertake to establish a favourable environment for investors whose projects are covered by their investment law (Mali, art. 8 and Guinea, art. 12), to ensure transparency of the investment framework and to protect against retroactive application of adverse laws (Liberia, Section 9 and 10) – which could all foster investment, including investment that could positively contribute to sustainable development. Others undertake to protect intellectual property rights in accordance with international agreements and treaties to which they are a party – which could thus foster innovation (Liberia, Section 8; Côte d'Ivoire, art. 32; and Benin, art. 14).

Most of these laws also contain provisions concerning the establishment and functioning of a specialised agency or commission to promote and facilitate investment, thus reinforcing the possibility of attracting investment that could positively contribute to sustainable development, although the extent to which these agencies prioritise sustainable investments is not assessed here.

Varying approaches to the availability of arbitration

All ECOWAS investment laws refer to arbitration for disputes with foreign and sometimes domestic investors but through different approaches. A first set of laws, including some more recent ones, provides advance government consent to arbitration, sometimes with limits on scope:

- Nigeria, Liberia and the Gambia's investment laws simply provide for arbitration (art. 26, 12 and 35 respectively);
- Cabo Verde provides that the dispute shall be settled by arbitration, if no other route has been agreed, or by the domestic courts if both parties agree to it (art. 14).
- Mali (art. 29), Benin (art. 45), Guinea-Bissau (art. 18-19) and Burkina Faso (art. 38-39) offer a choice between recourse to domestic courts or arbitration (and in certain cases conciliation) which specifies that initiation of arbitration suspends court proceedings.
- Niger authorises recourse to arbitration but limits it to certain disputes, i.e. those concerning the validity, interpretation, application or revision of one or several clauses in the certificate granting specific advantages (art. 45-47).

A second set of laws does not or does not appear to provide advance consent although other possible avenues are contemplated:

- Senegal (art. 12) provides that the dispute shall be settled in accordance with the conciliation and arbitration procedures resulting from an agreement between the parties or from agreements or treaties on the protection of investments concluded with the investor's home country – which suggests that if none exists, arbitration will not be possible.
- Sierra Leone and Ghana authorise recourse to arbitration and set out various procedural options but provide that "where no recourse is available through arbitration or previously established contracts or other legal instruments" (Sierra Leone) or if there is a disagreement with the investor as to the method of dispute settlement to be adopted, and if there is no arbitration agreement to the contrary (Ghana), the dispute shall be referred to the relevant legal authority (Sierra Leone) or resolved through mediation under Ghana's Alternative Dispute Resolution Act, 2010.
- Guinea and Togo provide that the dispute shall be settled by the domestic (or regional) courts but that the parties may agree to submit it to arbitration (art. 43 and 7 respectively).
- Côte d'Ivoire provides that UNCITRAL rules on conciliation shall apply to the dispute but that the parties may agree to submit their dispute to the arbitration centre of the Common Court of Justice and Arbitration of the OHADA. The investor is required to send a letter to the investment promotion agency which sets out the method of resolution chosen; by this choice the investor renounces the use of any other arbitration centre for the resolution of disputes with the state.

Table 2.1 summarises the foregoing discussion. It compares the provisions at the regional and continental level with those of national investment laws in ECOWAS member states as they relate to sustainable development. This summary of provisions in a binary fashion does not do full justice to the possible qualifications that might be included in any given provision, but overall it does provide a quick overview of the extent to which national investment laws fully reflect the innovations at regional and continental levels and which are most likely to be found in the forthcoming AfCFTA Investment Protocol.

Table 2.1. National investment laws in ECOWAS do not fully reflect broader continental approaches

	PAIC	SADC Model BIT	SADC PFI 2016	ECOWAS SA	ECOWIC	National investment laws
References to sustainable development, state's right to regulate or investor obligations in preamble or other general provisions	Yes	Yes	Yes	Yes	Yes	Yes = 7 No = 8
Limitations on the protection against expropriation (e.g public health, security and the environment)	Yes	Yes	Yes	Yes	Yes	Yes = 2 No = 13
National treatment	Yes	Yes	Yes	Yes		Yes = 11 No = 4
Limitations on NT, e.g when assessing "like circumstances"		Yes	Yes	Yes	Yes	Yes = 9 No = 2
Fair and equitable treatment (FET)	No	Either yes but qualified by customary international law or Fair Administrative Treatment	No	Yes (qualified by reference to CIL)	No	Yes (qualified) = 1 Yes (unqualified) = 1 No = 13
General exceptions for measures relating to sustainable development		Yes	No, except compliance with other treaties	Yes	Yes	
Compliance with domestic laws	Yes	Yes	Yes	Yes	Yes	Yes = 9 No = 6
Pre-establishment obligations (environment, labour, human rights, CSR, corruption)	Yes	Yes	No	Yes	Yes	Yes = 5 No = 10
Post-establishment obligations (environment, labour, human rights, CSR, corruption)	Yes	Yes	No	Yes	Yes	Yes = 12 No = 3

Source: OECD compilation

References

African Union (2019), *African Continental Free Trade Area Agreement*, https://au-afcfta.org/afcfta-legal-texts/. [3]

African Union (2016), *Pan-African Investment Code*, https://au.int/en/documents/20161231/pan-african-investment-code-paic. [7]

ECOWAS (2018), *ECOWAS Common Investment Code*, https://wacomp.projects.ecowas.int/wp-content/uploads/2020/03/ECOWAS-COMMON-INVESTMENT-CODEENGLISH.pdf. [6]

ECOWAS (2008), *Supplementary Act A/SA.3/12/08 Adopting Community Rules on Investment and the Modalities for their Implementation with ECOWAS*, https://ecowas.int/. [5]

Mbengue, M. and S. Schacherer (2021), "Evolution of International Investment Agreements in Africa: Features and Challenges of Investment Law "Africanization"", in *Handbook of International Investment Law and Policy*, Springer Singapore, Singapore, https://doi.org/10.1007/978-981-13-5744-2_77-2. [2]

OECD (2022), *FDI Qualities Policy Toolkit*, OECD Publishing, Paris, https://doi.org/10.1787/7ba74100-en. [1]

SADC (2018), *SADC Model BIT*, http://www.sadc.int/. [4]

SADC (2006), *Protocol on Finance and Investment 2006*, https://www.sadc.int/pillars/investment. [8]

3 Promoting sustainable investment

This chapter provides an overview of investment promotion agencies (IPAs) in ECOWAS Member States and on their main priorities and efforts to attract sustainable investment. It also draws on the experience of other regions to provide lessons on better targeting FDI to support sustainable development and sharpening the indicators used for this purpose.

Governments design investment promotion strategies to support the achievement of national development objectives through the promotion and facilitation of foreign direct investment (FDI). While sound investment policies are intended to ensure that host countries are attractive and FDI benefits are maximised, investment promotion strategies are designed to influence the kind of investment that is attracted. In this context, most governments prioritise certain types of investments over others, which takes place through the selection of priority sectors, source countries and investment projects (OECD, 2018[1]). This prioritisation occurs because some types of FDI, with certain characteristics, are considered to contribute more to a host country's development than other types (Sauvant and Mann, 2019[2]). In particular, the issues of sustainability, inclusiveness, and the contribution to the sustainable development goals (SDGs) have become increasingly important and have led some investment promotion agencies (IPAs) to redefine their priorities. This chapter provides an overview of IPAs in ECOWAS Member States and their main priorities and efforts to attract sustainable investment. It also draws on the experience of other regions to provide lessons on better targeting FDI to support sustainable development and refining the indicators used for this purpose.

Promoting and facilitating investment in ECOWAS

The role of national investment promotion agencies

Investment promotion strategies can be designed by the ministry in charge of investment, the investment promotion agency (IPA) or a combination of both or more actors. Whether key contributors or not, IPAs are the main implementors of their country's investment promotion strategies. All ECOWAS Member States have established an IPA, most of which have been recently created or restructured through governmental decrees. For instance, APIEX (Benin) was created in 2018, as the result of the merger of three state-owned companies in 2018. CEPICI (Côte d'Ivoire) was created in 1993 but underwent an institutional reform in 2012 while Cabo Verde TradeInvest was created in 2016 as the successor agency of Cabo Verde Investimentos. In some cases, agencies were created by executive decrees (Benin, Burkina Faso, Côte d'Ivoire, Guinea, Niger, Senegal, Togo) while in other instances they were established by legislative acts (the Gambia, Ghana, Liberia, Nigeria, Sierra Leone).

The structure and governance of IPAs differ across agencies in the region. Most are public autonomous agencies of an economic and administrative nature. Togo Invest is a state-owned company. Some agencies are placed under the direct supervision of the President or Prime Ministry's office, including in Benin, Côte d'Ivoire, Ghana, Liberia and Mali. Most IPAs have a board of directors, notably in Benin, Gambia, Ghana, Nigeria, Sierra Leone and Togo. Additionally, almost half of the IPAs in the region (Benin, Cabo Verde, Ghana, Guinea, Mali, Nigeria, Sierra Leone) have branch offices in other cities or regions beside the headquarters located in the capital city. The number of branch offices range from one in Sierra Leone to nine in Guinea.

While all IPAs in the region have the mandate to promote FDI into the country, some have additional mandates that go beyond investment. For example, a majority of IPAs in ECOWAS are also tasked to promote domestic investment, including Burkina Faso, Côte d'Ivoire, Ghana, Guinea, Liberia, Mali, Nigeria, Senegal and Togo. Promoting exports into foreign markets is also a mandate for the agencies of Benin, Cabo Verde, the Gambia and Sierra Leone. IPAs in the region offer different services to promote, attract and retain investment in their respective countries (Figure 3.1). The most frequent services provided by ECOWAS agencies are the provision of information on investment opportunities, support in setting up and expanding operations, organising matchmaking events and forums, and providing information and advice on the legal investment framework. Two thirds of IPAs host one-stop shops to centralise the process to establish a business and invest while GIEPA (the Gambia) is currently developing one.

Figure 3.1. Main services provided by ECOWAS IPAs

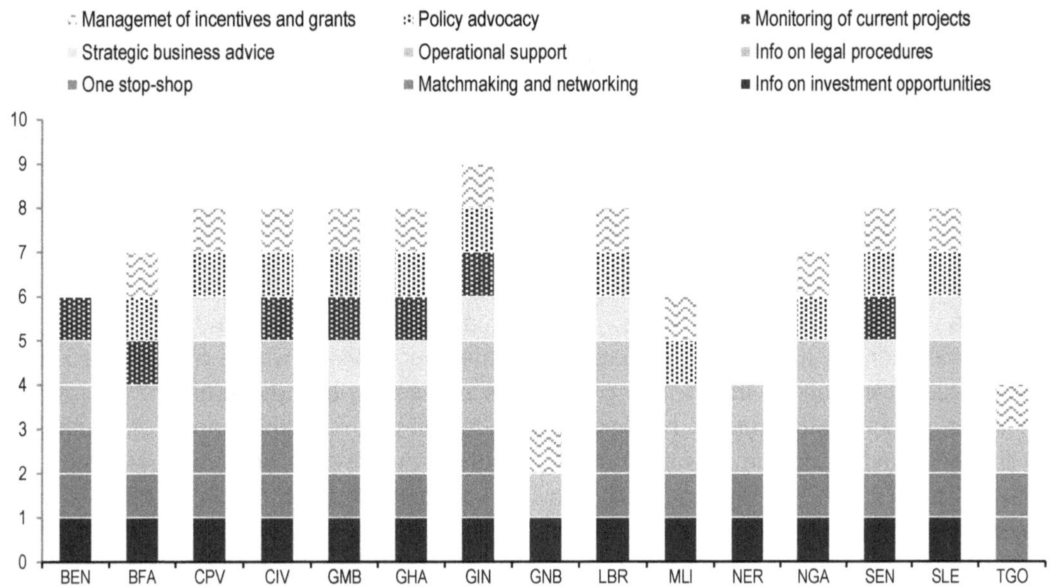

Source: OECD compilation based on IPAs' websites.

Promoting investment at regional level

In addition to the national IPAs, ECOWAS Member States are also seeking to co-ordinate their investment promotion and facilitation initiatives. The ECOWAS Investment Policy (ECOWIP), which is inspired by the OECD Policy Framework for Investment (OECD, 2015[3]), includes a chapter on the investment promotion and facilitation policy framework to support its Member States to adopt good international standards (ECOWAS, 2018[4]). Its main policy principles are the following:

- Pledge to create a regional IPA to co-ordinate investment-promotion and facilitation activities amongst the national IPAs of the Member States;
- Support the creation of national IPAs in those Member States in which none exists;
- Promote national IPAs that are autonomous and adequately funded and staffed, and that report directly to the highest political office in the relevant jurisdiction;
- Encourage one-stop investment facilitation mechanisms to minimise administrative and regulatory bottlenecks for investment-entry and doing business purposes;
- Facilitate national and regional collaboration to initiate reforms that translate into a more competitive regional investment climate in West Africa;
- Foster alliances with other regional and international investment-promotion networks;
- Encourage the establishment of national databases on investment; and
- Promote the publication of annual reports on investment inflows and outflows for each Member State, as well as all applicable national policies, laws regulations, and amendments.

How IPAs support the SDGs: experience from other regions

When governments design their investment promotion strategies, they prioritise certain types of sectors, countries, investment projects or individual investors – either because they have a higher probability of being realised or because they may bring certain benefits to the host economy (OECD, 2018[1]).

Prioritisation strategies can have different motivations, depending mostly on the country's national development objectives, local assets and international context. These strategies allow countries to specialise and target their FDI attraction efforts towards specific government priorities.

As IPAs recognise their role in attracting and boosting investment in support of the SDGs, they focus their efforts increasingly on those investors that are more likely to generate sustainable development impacts. In this light, this section provides a brief comparative analysis of the extent to which IPAs' investment promotion priorities contribute to sustainable development in member countries of two benchmark regions: the OECD and the Association of Southeast Asian Nations (ASEAN). The findings are based on the results of the *OECD survey on IPA Monitoring & Evaluation and Prioritisation*.

When asked about top factors influencing their investment promotion priorities, 56% of ASEAN IPAs rank jointly first the contribution to the SDGs, the political/national agenda and digital transformation (Figure 3.2). This share is higher than among OECD members (44%), where agencies adopt a rather pragmatic approach and select the results of previous monitoring and evaluation (M&E) as the most important factor. A robust M&E system can indeed capture different relevant aspects, including related to sustainability, and guide strategic orientations accordingly (Sztajerowska and Volpe Martincus, 2021[5]). The overall political or national agenda, which is also deemed important in both ASEAN and OECD countries, can underpin other factors as well, such as digitalisation and sustainability (OECD, 2023[6]).

Figure 3.2. Top factors motivating IPAs' current priorities in ASEAN and OECD countries

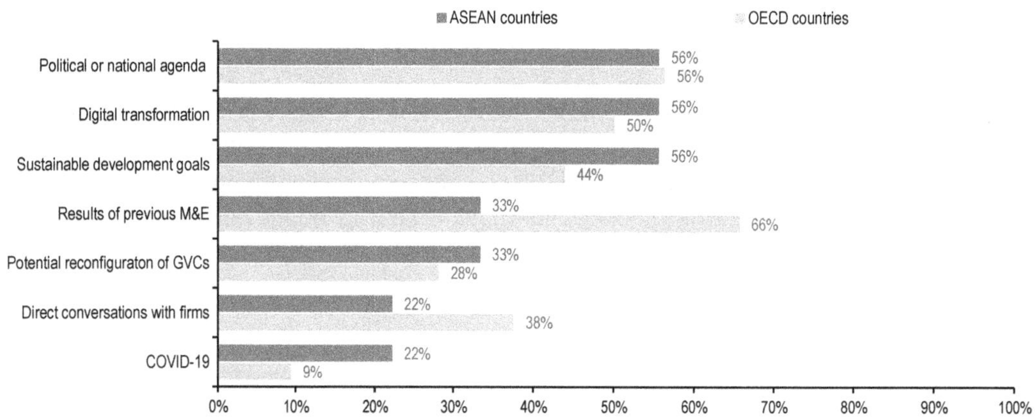

Source: OECD survey on IPA Monitoring & Evaluation and Prioritisation (OECD countries, 2021; ASEAN countries, 2022).

Conversely, the COVID-19 crisis is considered as a top factor by much fewer agencies. Although the pandemic has had a strong immediate effect on FDI flows and investment promotion activities around the world, prompting IPAs to change their priority actions and ways of working (OECD, 2020[7]), the crisis has not shifted their main concerns beyond key priorities such as sustainability and digitalisation. It has rather prompted governments and IPAs to accelerate their response to these global imperatives as a way to reinforce economic resilience.

As IPAs are increasingly targeting sustainable investment, they can contribute to some SDGs more than others. In both ASEAN and OECD countries, the SDGs relating to promoting economic growth and employment (Goal 8); supporting resilient infrastructure, industrialisation and innovation (Goal 9); and ensuring access to modern and clean energy (Goal 7) are mentioned by most IPAs (Figure 3.3). This is not a surprising result since these objectives correspond most closely to IPAs' usual tasks. ASEAN IPAs also focus more systematically than OECD IPAs on contributing to social and environmental sustainability, particularly good health and well-being (67%), sustainable cities and communities (67%), life on land (67%), poverty reduction (56%) and climate action (56%). ASEAN agencies are also more often integrated in the ministry in charge of investment or have a broader economic role, thereby giving them a wider field of action on key aspects related to the SDGs (OECD, 2023[6]). IPAs in the OECD are often more specialised and autonomous, focusing on selected tasks and priorities. IPAs in ECOWAS typically share a similar institutional profile to OECD agencies and may therefore display similar trends in terms of priorities. Preliminary evidence from a subset of ECOWAS countries that participated in the same survey shows that IPAs in the region prioritise the SDGs to a similar extent as OECD countries in their investment promotion strategies. The results also reveal that ECOWAS countries predominantly focus on the economic-oriented SDGs, particularly SDG 9, as well as SDGs 7 and 8, rather than the more sustainability-oriented ones.

Figure 3.3. The SDGs to which IPAs in ASEAN and OECD contribute

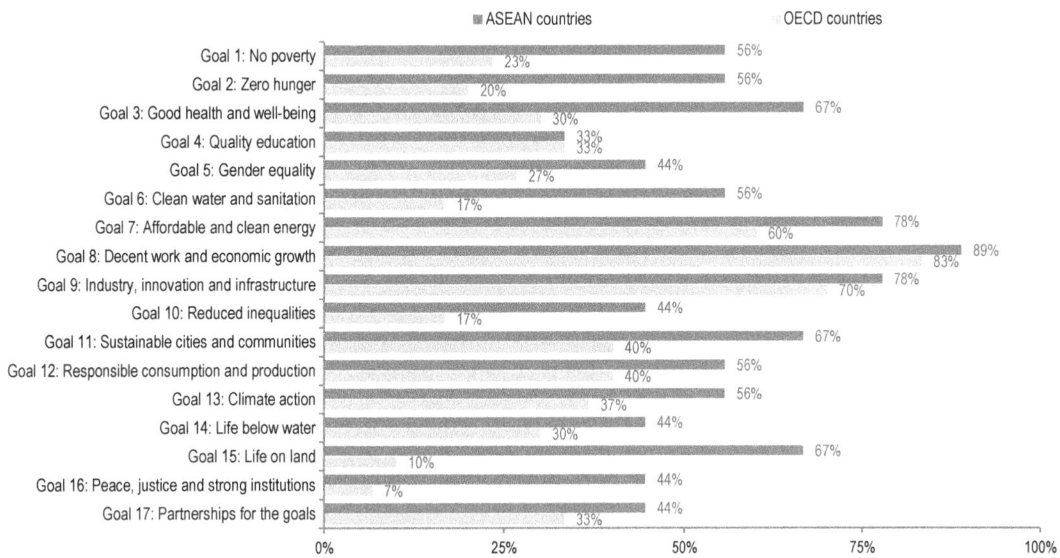

Source: OECD survey on IPA Monitoring & Evaluation and Prioritisation (OECD countries, 2021; ASEAN countries, 2022).

Priority sectors and sustainability in ECOWAS

Like IPAs in the OECD and ASEAN regions, agencies in ECOWAS seek to prioritise certain sectors over others in their investment promotion efforts. Agriculture is promoted by all IPAs. Other highly promoted sectors include construction and infrastructure; energy; technology and communication; and tourism and hospitality (Table 3.1). IPAs also promote specific sectors, such as the creative industry in Cabo Verde, the iron and steel industry in the Gambia and retail, timber and brewing industries in Nigeria. While the IPAs from Benin and Ghana promote the largest array of sectors on their websites, those from Mali, Senegal and Sierra Leone are the most selective.

Several agencies in the region put a particular emphasis on promoting sustainable investment, especially through the promotion of specific sectors such as renewable energy. The IPAs from Benin, Burkina Faso, Cabo Verde, the Gambia, Ghana, Guinea, Mali, Niger, Sierra Leone and Togo list the promotion of FDI in renewable energy sectors on their websites. But only a few provide detailed information on investment opportunities in these sectors and related incentives and legal background (Cabo Verde, the Gambia, Ghana, Mali and Sierra Leone). In some cases, these measures are part of broader overarching sustainable development strategies. The Gambia, for example, focuses particularly on attracting large-scale projects in the solar energy sector as part of a broader strategy to develop the solar energy industry. Some of the priorities of Cabo Verde's IPA are guided by the *Ambição 2030 - Declaration of Commitment for Sustainable Development*. In Sierra Leone, attracting FDI in the renewable energy sector aims to support the country's strategic vision to make it Africa's first zero-carbon middle-income economy by 2040. The IPA of Niger is seeking to attract investment that can support the country's Economic and Social Development Plan, including its "sustainable management of the environment" axis.

Table 3.1. Main sectors promoted by ECOWAS IPAs

	BEN	BFA	CPV	CIV	GMB	GHA	GIN	GNB	LBR	MLI	NER	NGA	SEN	SLE	TGO
Agriculture	■	■	■	■	■	■	■	■	■	■	■	■	■	■	■
Construction / infrastructure	■	■	■	■		■	■	■	■	■	■				■
Education		■				■									
Energy	■	■	■	■	■	■	■			■	■	■		■	■
Incl. renewable energy	■	■	■		■	■	■			■	■			■	■
Finance / insurance						■					■	■			■
Fishing	■		■	■				■	■				■	■	■
Health / pharmaceutical		■		■		■							■		
Livestock	■	■						■	■	■	■	■			
Manufacturing	■	■	■	■	■	■		■	■		■	■			
Mining	■	■		■		■	■		■		■		■		■
Technology / communication	■	■	■		■	■	■	■	■		■	■	■		■
Textile / garments	■	■	■		■	■					■	■			
Tourism / hospitality	■	■	■		■	■	■	■			■		■	■	■
Trade / commerce	■							■							
Transport / logistics	■		■		■	■			■		■				■

Source: OECD compilation based on IPAs' websites.

Côte d'Ivoire, for its part, is focused on attracting FDI in waste management and recycling, more particularly in: (i) plastic waste recycling for the manufacture of packaging, (ii) cardboard and paper recycling, (iii) paper production based on cellulosic waste, (iv) used broken glass recycling, and (v) hollow and pressed glass manufacturing. Senegal does not focus its attraction efforts on the renewable energy sector but seeks to make some of its target sectors more sustainable, notably by attracting sustainable mining projects and ecotourism investors. Togo aims to attract investment in an aquaculture project that favours an environmentally friendly and long-term sustainable fish farming model.

IPAs should not only focus on promoting sustainable investment through new investments, but also use the SDGs to guide them in the way they deliver investment facilitation and aftercare services to existing investors who wish to expand or reinvest. IPAs in ECOWAS could, for example, consider focusing aftercare activities on those investors with the highest sustainability impacts. They could also take advantage of these services to better promote responsible business conduct within the existing business community and encourage investors to comply with sustainability-related laws more systematically, as well as to embrace responsible practices in their business operations (see Section on Responsible Business Conduct).

Indicators to prioritise and measure sustainability outcomes of FDI

A key question is the way and degree to which IPAs can track their contribution to national sustainable development objectives, beyond the actual sectors they target. A closer look at their key performance indicators (KPIs) is necessary to understand and evaluate the extent to which investment promotion strategies contribute to attracting and facilitating sustainable investment. IPAs need to rely on specific and consistent indicators to ensure that: (i) they attract the right investments, and (ii) the attracted FDI actually generates sustainability outcomes.

To select priority firms and guide their decision on whether to assist a particular investment project, IPAs rely on KPIs related to outcomes, some of which aim to assess the contribution of a project to local development and sustainable growth. These can be grouped into several broad categories. The most used KPIs in both ASEAN and OECD countries are those relating to productivity and innovation, and those on job quantity and quality (Figure 3.4). This is likely to be the case in ECOWAS as well, as these are the prime objectives of IPAs.

Figure 3.4. Types of KPIs used for FDI prioritisation by ASEAN and OECD agencies

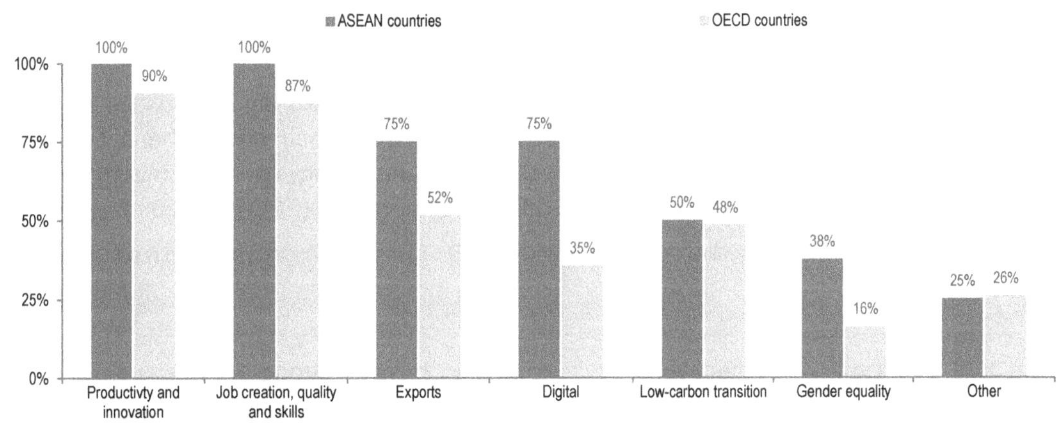

Source: OECD survey on IPA Monitoring & Evaluation and Prioritisation (OECD, 2021; ASEAN, 2022).

IPAs can also use KPIs that are related to the SDGs but do not appear in the categories in the figure. For example, the Philippines uses indicators to prioritise investment projects that have a positive impact on nature conservation and the protection of sea and coastline. Similarly, Indonesia uses a different type of prioritisation indicator relating to the geographical dispersion of FDI and measured by the value of investment realisations outside Java (OECD, 2023[6]). Promoting investment in support of regional development has also become a high priority in OECD countries. As 92% of agencies have the mandate to promote and facilitate FDI in support of regional development, 69% use FDI distribution across regions as a KPI (OECD, 2022[8]).

KPIs related to the low-carbon transition are used by approximately half of the agencies for FDI prioritisation in ASEAN and OECD countries. Indicators to prioritise low-carbon FDI can be very diverse from one agency to the other – depending on the priorities but also the resources and capacities of these agencies – and are often still in development. Several more sophisticated mechanisms are emerging and increasingly used, however (Box 3.1).

Box 3.1. Environmental sustainability KPIs for prioritisation in selected ASEAN and OECD IPAs

Different indicators have been developed and are used differently by IPAs. Many of them set a target and track the number of attracted and realised projects according to their target sectors and countries.

IDA Ireland has set a target to win 60 environmental sustainability investments in 2021-24. In identifying priority investments, IDA has developed an approach guided by the six sustainable activities set out in the European Union taxonomy on sustainable investment and by an analysis of the sustainability opportunities which align with Ireland's core strengths, and which are deemed to present the greatest opportunity to win FDI.

Business Sweden has embraced the long-term national 'Pioneer the Fossil Free' initiative, by setting clear objectives to accelerate green investments to Sweden to become fossil free by 2045. The agency identifies companies, solutions and expertise that can support reducing CO2 emissions in Sweden and monitors and adapts its investment promotion priorities and activities accordingly.

The *Malaysian Investment Development Authority* targets companies that adopt green technologies and the reuse and recycling of activities, as well as projects applying the circular economy model (e.g. pollution and waste management) to prioritise investment. The *Philippine Board of Investments* uses indicators to prioritise investors with green processes and the use of modern and clean technology.

Some agencies are also developing sustainability scoring mechanisms. For example, *Germany Trade & Invest* developed an integrated scoring model, where FDI projects are assessed and scored against a set of qualitative and quantitative indicators for sustainability. The agency then adjusts its promotion and advisory services to investors accordingly. Similarly, *Invest in Canada* has recently introduced a scoring mechanism to prioritise investment opportunities based on two dimensions: FDI impact and investment potential. The former evaluates the likelihood that the investment will benefit Canada and one variable focuses on social and sustainable development. The agency uses Bloomberg terminal and its scoring system to measure Environmental, Social and Governance (ESG) related impact.

Source: OECD survey on IPA monitoring & evaluation and prioritisation (OECD countries, 2021); direct interactions with IPAs.

To ensure that prioritisation is effective, it is important to have a strong M&E system with relevant indicators. While it is key to prioritise certain investments over others to respond to sustainability objectives, it is equally important to understand and track their contribution to the desired outcomes. Integrating sustainability indicators in IPA M&E systems is necessary to measure the results of the agency and the effective contribution of companies assisted by the IPA to sustainable development, including the decarbonisation of the economy. In OECD countries, many IPAs still tend to rely predominantly, or exclusively, on metrics relating to the number and value of investment projects or on the number of jobs created (Sztajerowska and Volpe Martincus, 2021[5]).

Some agencies, however, increasingly pay more attention to sustainability-related KPIs and track the number of projects in relation to their priority sectors. For example, the Turkish IPA measures the number of projects that are realised in the targeted low-carbon sectors, namely recycling, renewable energy, and the development of energy efficient components and technologies. The Finnish agency has introduced an impact assessment mechanism based on direct interviews with investors. Advisors from the agency ask questions to representatives of any new investment project dealing with their carbon impact. The answers provided allow them to formulate outcome indicators on the contribution of the investments attracted to the country's low-carbon transition.

To conclude, in their efforts to achieve the SDGs through FDI, ECOWAS Member States need to ensure that the actual indicators used by their IPAs to prioritise investments and to measure their outcomes are aligned with the overarching investment promotion priorities. Effective sustainable investment promotion strategies require granular indicators and measurements. Additionally, KPIs used for M&E should ideally be aligned with those used for prioritisation to ensure consistency between the set targets and the desired outcomes.

References

ECOWAS (2018), *ECOWAS Investment Policy*, https://wacomp.projects.ecowas.int/wp-content/uploads/2020/03/ECOWAS-INVESTMENT-POLICY-ENGLISH.pdf. [4]

OECD (2023), “Enabling sustainable investment in ASEAN”*, OECD Business and Finance Policy Papers*, No. 23, OECD Publishing, Paris, https://doi.org/10.1787/eb34f287-en. [6]

OECD (2022), “The geography of foreign investment in OECD member countries: How investment promotion agencies support regional development”*, OECD Business and Finance Policy Papers*, No. 20, OECD Publishing, Paris, https://doi.org/10.1787/1f293a25-en. [8]

OECD (2020), *Investment promotion agencies in the time of COVID-19*, https://read.oecd-ilibrary.org/view/?ref=132_132715-6ewiabvnx7&title=Investment-promotion-agencies-in-the-time-of-COVID-19. [7]

OECD (2018), *Mapping of Investment Promotion Agencies in OECD Countries*, https://www.oecd.org/investment/investment-policy/mapping-of-investment-promotion-agencies-in-OECD-countries.pdf. [1]

OECD (2015), *Policy Framework for Investment, 2015 Edition*, OECD Publishing, Paris, https://doi.org/10.1787/9789264208667-en. [3]

Sauvant, K. and H. Mann (2019), “Making FDI More Sustainable: Towards an Indicative List of FDI Sustainability Characteristics”, *Journal of World Investment & Trade*, Vol. vol. 20 (Dec. 2019), pp. pp.916-952, https://ssrn.com/abstract=3509771. [2]

Sztajerowska, M. and C. Volpe Martincus (2021), *Together or Apart: Investment Promotion Agencies' Prioritisation and Monitoring and Evaluation for Sustainable Investment Promotion*, OECD Investment Insights, Paris, https://www.oecd.org/daf/inv/investment-policy/Investment-Insights-Investment-Promotion-Prioritisation-OECD.pdf. [5]

4 Assessing use and design of investment incentives

This chapter looks at tax incentive design and policy goals within ECOWAS and compared to peer regions, based on an analysis of CIT incentives in selected ECOWAS Member States. The analysis is based on comparable data from the OECD Investment Tax Incentive Database, covering CIT incentives across 52 developing and emerging countries.

ECOWAS governments offer a range of tax incentives in an effort to attract private investment and direct it into certain sectors and locations or encourage certain activities. While tax incentives may promote investment with potential positive effects on output, employment, productivity, or other objectives related to the Sustainable Development Goals (SDGs), their net benefits are often not well understood. Tax incentives reduce revenue-raising capacity, and can create economic distortions, increase administrative and compliance costs, and increase tax competition. Striking the right balance between a tax regime that supports domestic and foreign investment and securing the necessary revenues for public spending is a challenge for policymakers, particularly in developing countries, where corporate income tax (CIT) revenues are often an important source of public finances.

This chapter looks at tax incentive design and policy goals within ECOWAS and compared to peer regions, based on an analysis of CIT incentives in seven ECOWAS Member States – Côte d'Ivoire, Gambia, Ghana, Liberia, Nigeria, Senegal, and Sierra Leone. The analysis is based on comparable data from the OECD Investment Tax Incentive Database, covering CIT incentives across 52 developing and emerging economies (Box 4.1). Granular and comprehensive data are indispensable to improve our understanding of existing tax incentive policies and to enhance the analysis of their impacts, particularly given that their effectiveness and costs are strongly design- and context-specific. Analysis on incentive design can inform assessments of whether incentives support positive economic, social and environmental spillovers, and at what costs.

Box 4.1. OECD Investment Tax Incentives Database

To better understand how tax incentives are used across countries, the OECD Investment Tax Incentives Database (ITID) systematically compiles quantitative and qualitative information on the design of CIT incentives, using a consistent data collection methodology. For each tax incentive, it includes information along three dimensions: instrument-specific design features, eligibility conditions and legal basis. This allows for cross-country comparisons on how countries design their tax incentives and what types of business and project characteristics they target. As of October 2022, the database covered 52 developing economies in Eurasia, the Middle East and North Africa, Southeast Asia, Sub-Saharan African and includes five LAC economies. Celani, Dressler and Wermelinger (2022[1]) present the methodology and key classifications underlying the OECD ITID as well as its scope. The regional groups and corresponding countries included in this report the following:

- *Association of Southeast Asian Nations (ASEAN)*: Cambodia, Indonesia, Lao PDR, Malaysia, Myanmar, Philippines, Thailand, Viet Nam.
- *Eastern Partnership (EaP)*: Armenia, Azerbaijan, Georgia, Moldova, Ukraine.
- *Economic Community of West African States (ECOWAS)*: Cote d'Ivoire, Gambia, Ghana, Liberia, Nigeria, Senegal, Sierra Leone.
- *Latin America and the Caribbean (LAC)*: Argentina, Brazil, Dominican Republic, Jamaica, and Paraguay.
- *Southern African Development Community* (SADC): Comoros, Democratic Republic of the Congo, Eswatini, Lesotho, Madagascar, Mozambique, Mauritius, Malawi, Namibia, Tanzania, South Africa, Zambia, Zimbabwe.

Source: Celani, Dressler and Wermelinger (2022[1]), https://doi.org/10.1787/62e075a9-en; OECD (2022[2]), www.oecd.org/investment/investment-policy/oecd-investment-tax-incentives-database-2022-update-brochure.pdf.

Investment tax incentives: opportunities and challenges

In a context of low and stagnant foreign direct investment (FDI) to ECOWAS Member States, most governments consider investment tax incentives (primarily tax but also financial, in-kind and regulatory benefits) as a key tool to promote FDI. The benefits and costs of granting tax incentives are not always clear. In the best case, tax incentives can attract investors that would not otherwise enter the market, help correct market failures, and encourage positive spillovers of investment on the economy, society or for the environment. In the worst of cases, incentives result in windfall gains to projects that would have materialised also without the incentive, encourage rent-seeking behaviour and contribute to economic distortions, while costing the state significant resources in revenue forgone, which could be used to advance development aims. Assessing the benefits of incentives and whether they outweigh their direct and indirect costs is not always straightforward.

Whether tax incentives are effective at attracting investors or encouraging positive investor behaviour depends on the country context including the wider investment climate, the investor and project sensitivity to incentives over other location determinants, and the design of the incentive regime (Box 4.2). Investment tax incentives are one, and often not the determining, factor for firms' investment location decisions, and cannot compensate for a weak investment climate (Van Parys and James, 2010[3]; Klemm and Van Parys, 2012[4]). Governments nonetheless often use incentives in place of more difficult reforms, for example, as a way around inefficient tax administration burdens faced by businesses. According to one estimate, firms spend on average nearly 270 hours to comply with taxes in ECOWAS (double the time spent in OECD countries). This incentivises firms to seek, and governments to grant, tax exemptions to avoid such long and costly procedures. However, this perpetuates unequal treatment of tax payers that might create distortions (PwC, 2020[5]; ECOWAS-UEMOA, 2022[6]).

Box 4.2. Context matters for tax incentive effectiveness

In addition to incentive design (covered throughout this chapter), the effect of tax incentives on investment depends on the characteristics of the investor and country-specific context. Some investors appear to be more sensitive to incentives than others. Projects that privilege low-cost production sites, including some export-oriented manufacturing, and investors that are highly mobile can rank incentives high on factors for location decisions. Other investors, such as those interested in the domestic market or natural resources, appear less swayed by incentives (James, 2014[7]; Andersen, Kett and von Uexkull, 2018[8]).

But investor response varies by country. Several empirical studies found no effect of tax incentives on FDI attraction in many countries in sub-Saharan Africa (Klemm and Van Parys, 2012[4]; Van Parys and James, 2010[3]; Ghrara and El Morchid, 2022[9]). In many developing countries, the quality of infrastructure and the regulatory framework are cited by investors as more important factors in determining their investment location decision than tax benefits (UNIDO, 2013[10]; IMF-OECD, 2017[11]). While lower effective tax rates are associated with higher FDI flows, this effect is significantly stronger in countries with good investment climates, and can have almost no effect in economies with weak investment climates, underlining the importance of wider reforms for FDI attraction (James, 2014[7]).

In general, evidence suggests that while tax benefits can play a role in some investment decisions, they may not be the most effective or efficient policy instrument to stimulate investment (IMF-OECD-UN-World Bank, 2015[12]). Competition between countries means that many incentives are overly generous, with costs outweighing the marginal impact on investment (Chai and Goyal, 2008[13]). This makes monitoring and evaluating incentive policy key.

Across sub-Saharan Africa, the scope of CIT incentives has contributed to an overall narrowing of the CIT base (Keen and Mansour, 2009[14]; Abbas and Klemm, 2013[15]). Statutory CIT rates in the selected ECOWAS countries are between 25 and 30%, which is similar to other developing and emerging regions covered by the database (OECD, 2023[16]; Tax Foundation, 2022[17]). Yet, incentives can reduce these rates substantially, and many companies may be eligible for them. Analysis of effective average tax rates (EATRs) in seven Sub-Saharan African countries found that tax incentives reduce EATRs by 30% on average in the sectors considered. The most generous tax treatment is typically offered within SEZs, where tax incentives on average lowered EATRs by 65% compared to the standard tax treatment. In some specific cases, including in Eswatini and Mauritius, tax incentives can reduce EATRs to nearly zero (Celani, Dressler and Hanappi, 2022[18]).[1]

Meanwhile, tax revenues are a key source of public finances, crucial for delivering public goods and services, including infrastructure, education and skills development – factors that also affect the country's investment climate. Extensive tax relief for investment projects might limit mobilising domestic resources necessary for progressing towards the SDGs. Among West African Economic and Monetary Union countries (UEMOA) the average tax-to-GDP ratio is 13.4% (2019), below the 20% regional target set by the IMF, and has not risen over the past decade (IMF, 2021[19]).

The estimated costs of tax incentives are often not transparent, due in part to limited reporting. In the median country in Africa where data are available, tax expenditures (estimated revenue forgone) from CIT incentives represent around 0.2% of GDP. This is similar to rates in Asia and Europe, however the impact on total taxes is greater, as CIT revenues (as a percentage of total tax revenues) are almost four times as high as in Europe. According to data from the Global Tax Expenditures Database (GTED) and OECD revenue statistics, about a quarter of African countries for which data are available have tax expenditures that are almost double the median rate, suggesting a substantial impact on government finances in terms of forgone revenue (OECD, 2022[20]). The GTED also suggests that in several ECOWAS Member States

VAT and excise tax incentives cost more in revenue forgone than CIT incentives (Redonda, von Haldenwang and Aliu, 2022[21]). This shows the importance of looking at the full scope of tax benefits available to investors in considering both the costs of incentives and their policy goals.[2]

Many governments are aware of the costs of incentives and unclear benefits, but face high pressure to offer generous tax incentives, internally from firms lobbying for advantages and externally from other countries with expansive incentive packages. This makes analysis on the scope, goals and design of incentives key, as improving design can help limit redundancies and encourage positive spillovers. Conditioning incentives on specific outcomes or promoting these outcomes through other eligibility criteria, while limiting the generosity of some incentives can be an important step in this regard. While outcome conditions can promote positive spillovers of investment, they require careful monitoring to ensure that the outcome has been met. This necessitates resources, administrative capacity, and close coordination with other government agencies. It is expected that the global minimum tax, agreed by 138 jurisdictions, will also help curb harmful tax competition, and encourage better incentive design (Box 4.4).

Tax incentive design in ECOWAS: insights from the OECD ITID

Tax incentive design is a key factor determining the benefits and costs of incentives. It relates to how the incentive reduces taxation (the instrument, the qualifying income and expenditures it applies to, and other features, Box 4.3), eligibility conditions (which investors and projects qualify to receive the incentive), and governance (how the incentive is awarded to investors) (Celani, Dressler and Wermelinger, 2022[1]). These policy design choices determine incentive targeting, investor uptake and behaviour, the extent to which incentives contribute to stated policy goals, and at what cost. The OECD ITID provides insights into how seven ECOWAS Member States use and grant incentives, which policy goals can be derived from incentive design, and how these practices compare with other regional groups. This analysis should be considered in conjunction with other chapters of this review, including how incentives factor into investment promotion strategies and whether incentives are prevalent in sectors already receiving FDI.

Box 4.3. Common tax incentive instruments

Investment tax incentives provide favourable deviations from the standard tax treatment for a specific group of corporate taxpayers, based on sector, activity, location or other investor- or project-related characteristics. Most countries provide preferential CIT treatment through four main instruments:

Tax exemptions provide a full or partial exemption of qualifying taxable income, which may refer to all of a business' income or income from particular sources (e.g. export income).

Reduced rates provide CIT rates below the standard (statutory) rate for qualifying taxable income.

Tax allowances and **tax credits** allow firms to deduct a certain share of qualifying capital or current expenditure from taxable income (tax allowances) or directly from taxes due (tax credits). Qualifying capital expenditures are generally asset specific (e.g., machinery, buildings, equipment). Qualifying current expenditure tends to be activity specific (e.g., spending on training, R&D, exporting). Tax allowances on capital expenditure can accelerate or enhance the deduction of capital costs. Tax allowances that accelerate the deduction of capital costs allow for the faster recovery of the cost of an asset, while tax allowances that enhance deductions apply in addition to standard capital deductions and result in deductions that effectively exceed the initial capital cost. Tax allowances on current expenditures and tax credits can result in deductions that effectively exceed original expenses (for example, a 200% tax allowance on employee training).

The first two instruments (tax exemptions and reduced rates) are **income-based incentives**; they provide tax relief based on earnings. Tax allowances and credits are **expenditure-based incentives** because they lower the cost of capital or certain spending.

Source: Celani, Dressler and Wermelinger (2022[11]) https://doi.org/10.1787/62e075a9-en.

Full tax exemptions are prevalent in ECOWAS Member States

While income-based incentives (i.e. CIT exemptions and reduced rates) are widely used across developing economies, these incentives are not always effective in attracting new investment, and have substantial costs – including forgone tax revenue, economic distortions and increased tax competition – which could outweigh their benefits (IMF-OECD-UN-World Bank, 2015[12]; James, 2014[7]; Zee, Stotsky and Ley, 2002[22]). Income-based incentives disproportionately benefit projects that are already profitable early in the tax relief period, making projects that would materialise without the incentive even more profitable (Box 4.3). Full tax exemptions are particularly costly, and can result in a race-to-the-bottom tax competition with other economies over mobile foreign investment, while potentially generating windfall gains for projects that would have taken place in absence of the incentives (Klemm and Van Parys, 2012[4]; James, 2014[7]). Tax exemptions and reduced CIT rates are likely to be particularly affected by the global minimum tax (Box 4.4).

There is evidence suggesting potential positive effects of expenditure-based incentives on investment in certain conditions (House and Shapiro, 2008[23]; Appelt, González Cabral and Hanappi, 2022[24]). Because expenditure-based incentives directly target investment expenses, they reduce the cost of capital, making investments more profitable at the margin (IMF, OECD, UN, World Bank, 2015[25]). The benefit for the company depends on the size of the investment it undertakes and can also be linked to specific activities and policy objectives (e.g. R&D, skills development etc.). These incentives therefore lend themselves to improving the positive impact of investment on sustainable development (OECD, 2022[26]). Additional research is required to assess impacts in different contexts. Expenditure-based incentives typically have higher administrative costs, and if not well designed can favour existing companies more than new ventures with low profits (UN-CIAT, 2018[27]; Morisset and Pirnia, 1999[28]). All incentives require comprehensive monitoring and evaluation to assess their costs and benefits.

Box 4.4. Tax incentives and the global minimum tax for MNEs

The recently agreed Global Minimum Tax for large MNEs places multilaterally limits to tax competition that contribute to the erosion of domestic tax bases. Pillar Two of the two-pillar solution agreed by 138 members of the Inclusive Framework on Base Erosion and Profit Shifting requires large MNEs (with revenues above USD 750 million) to pay a 15% minimum effective tax rate in all jurisdictions in which they operate. This means that if there are affiliates of an in scope MNEs with an effective tax rates (ETR) below 15%, top-up taxes may be due. In the absence of tax reform or other policy actions, governments could potentially forgo such revenues arising from low-taxed profit in their jurisdiction that would be collected by other jurisdictions.

As more countries are moving to implement the global minimum tax, it is important for ECOWAS Member States to analyse the implications of the global minimum tax on domestic tax systems. The GloBE Rules will not affect all jurisdictions, MNEs and tax incentives in the same manner. The impact of the GloBE Rules on tax incentives will depend on their design, on the jurisdiction's tax system (its baseline tax system and its use of base narrowing provisions), and on the characteristics of MNEs and the activities they perform in the jurisdiction.

The impact of the GloBE Rules will strongly depend on the design of tax incentives. OECD analysis shows that income-based incentives for in-scope MNEs will be strongly affected, whereas expenditure-based incentives are less likely to be affected, with some incentives such as accelerated depreciation for tangible assets affected only to a limited extent. The new rules allow a carve-out for profits associated with economic substance (the substance-based income exclusion, SBIE), which allows 5% of the value of tangible assets and payroll to be subtracted from the profits to which the top-up tax applies. This means that tax incentives that are successful in attracting tangible assets and generating employment will be less affected from the minimum tax.

Governments are strongly advised to consider the implications of the minimum tax on their tax incentives. It will be important to ensure coordination across ministries on this issue given the fast pace of action of reform in this area.

Source: (OECD, 2022[20]), https://doi.org/10.1787/25d30b96-en.

Most of the ECOWAS countries considered offer CIT exemptions (Figure 4.1). Income-based CIT incentives (CIT exemptions and reduced CIT rates) are frequently used in ECOWAS and amount to 61% of registered incentives. Full CIT exemptions are available in all but two of the countries considered, and account for over a third of all incentives offered in the region. Sierra Leone only offers full CIT exemptions, some of which are permanent. All other countries examined provide a mix of income and expenditure-based incentives (i.e. tax allowances and credits) and three (Côte d'Ivoire, Nigeria and Liberia) grant mostly or only expenditure-based benefits. Countries in ECOWAS are as likely to have expenditure-based incentives as in ASEAN, for example. They are less likely to use tax allowances than SADC or LAC countries covered in the database. Typically, expenditure-based incentives are more commonly used by countries with higher income levels given their greater capacity requirements in terms of administration and compliance monitoring, although exceptions exist.

While many countries (across regions) offer permanent low CIT rates for certain sectors, these benefits are costly in terms of revenue forgone as well as potential long-term economic distortions. Stability is important to investors, but when incentive recipients gain permanent preferential treatment vis-à-vis competitors, incentives can become a tool for rent-seeking (Abramovsky et al., 2018[29]) (Lent, 1967[30]). Permanently reduced rates should be assessed for generosity compared to the statutory rate. Temporary incentives, and especially full CIT exemptions, also have costs and risks, including that firms may leave the jurisdiction when the incentive expires. Some firms may also seek to continue receiving the incentive after their benefit has lapsed, such as by incorporating a new firm that qualifies for the tax exemption, resulting in de-facto permanent incentives (IMF-OECD-UN-World Bank, 2015[12]).

Figure 4.1. Income-based incentives are prevalent in ECOWAS

% of countries in region offering at least one incentive

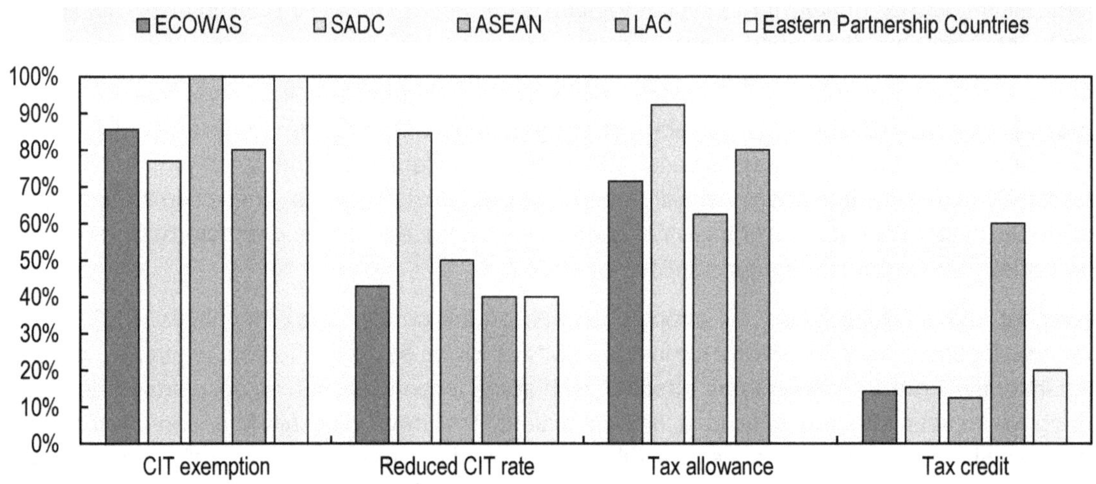

Note: See Box 4.1 for information on countries covered in each regional group. The number of registered incentives in each region is: 128 (SADC), 69 (ECOWAS), 78 (ASEAN), 19 (EaP), 35 (LAC).
Source: OECD ITID, April 2023, based on 52 economies and 464 CIT incentive entries.

Income-based incentives granted in selected ECOWAS Member States are mostly temporary; for example, in Nigeria export-oriented firms are fully exempt from CIT for three years. More than half of income-based incentives in the ECOWAS Member States are granted for periods of five to ten years. More than one-quarter are granted permanently (Figure 4.2). The duration of incentives is similar to SADC and ASEAN, though ASEAN offers more short-term incentives (under five years) and very few permanent benefits. The trend across incentives is similar across ECOWAS; most of the seven countries considered offer all or most income-based incentives for up to ten years. Three countries offer permanent income-based incentives (Ghana, Senegal and Sierra Leone). For example, Ghana offers permanently reduced CIT rates for certain manufacturing companies and hotels, and for income from exports of non-traditional goods.[3] Senegal's income-based incentives all apply on a permanent basis and include partial CIT exemptions for exporters and renewable energy, and reduced CIT rates in economic zones.

Sunset clauses, which stipulate an end date to an incentive policy unless legislative action is taken to extend the benefit, can help contain the cost of incentive regimes. Indeed time-bound incentives may be easier to remove, as politically it is often more difficult for governments to end incentives than to introduce new ones. Moreover, they can facilitate monitoring and evaluation, as the merits of an incentive can be assessed after a fixed period to determine whether the incentive should be continued, reformed or left to expire, particularly if evaluation requirements are in the law. Lastly, there is some evidence that expenditure-based tax incentives with sunset clauses have a greater effect on investment attraction than permanent benefits, since investors are encouraged to act quickly to enjoy the benefit (Wen, 2020[31]; US Department of the Treasury, 2010[32]). However, governments must clearly communicate if incentives are time-bound, as sunset clauses can introduce an element of uncertainty for investors. Based on the OECD ITID, only two incentives offered by the ECOWAS Member States covered in the database have sunset clauses: a three-year tourism tax exemption in Sierra Leone; and an enhanced tax allowance on qualifying assets for manufacturing and service sectors in Liberia.

Figure 4.2. Most income-based incentives granted for 5-10 years, many are permanent

Duration of income-based incentives, as a share of total number of income-based incentives in each region (as covered by the database)

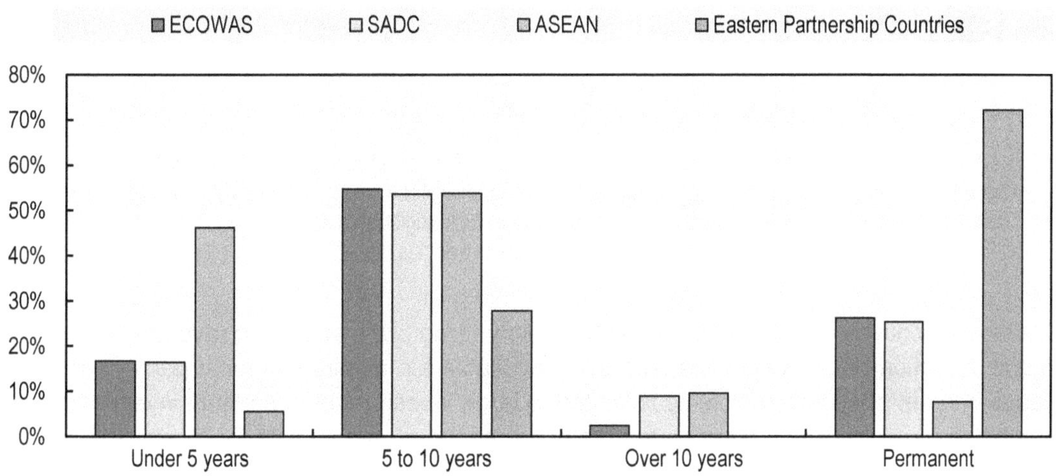

Note: See Box 4.1 for information on countries covered in each regional group. The graph reflects durations of CIT exemptions and reduced CIT rates. The number of income-based incentives reflected in each region is: 42 (ECOWAS), 67 (SADC), 52 (ASEAN), 18 (EaP).
Source: OECD ITID, April 2023, based on 52 economies and 464 CIT incentive entries.

Eligibility conditions suggest a focus on large investors in key sectors

Incentive eligibility conditions are criteria that businesses or investment projects must meet to receive a tax benefit. Incentive policies often tie tax support to investment in specific sectors or locations, or certain investor or project characteristics (e.g., majority foreign-owned, minimum project investment value, new entrant). Incentives are also often conditional on certain investor activities (e.g. training, R&D) or outcomes (e.g. job creation, energy efficiency) (Celani, Dressler and Wermelinger, 2022[1]). Among the ECOWAS Member states covered, sector-related criteria are by far the most common: all ECOWAS countries examined have at least one CIT incentive requiring investors to operate in a certain sector (Figure 4.3, Panel A). The use of sector-based conditions is also commonly observed in other regions. More than half of all incentives covered in the OECD ITID require investors to meet multiple eligibility conditions (Figure 4.3, Panel B). Most often, sector conditions are combined with location, outcome or minimum investment size conditions.

Figure 4.3. Nearly all incentives target certain sectors, most require multiple eligibility conditions

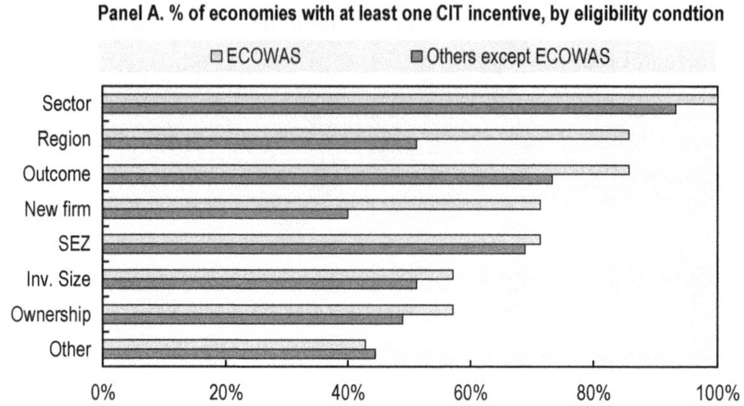

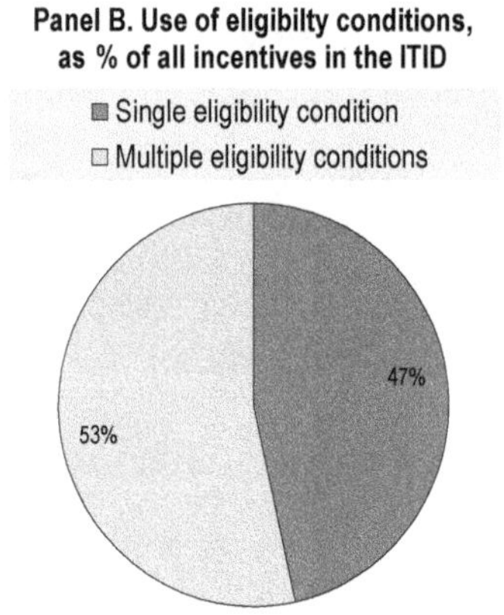

Note: See Box 4.1 for information on countries covered in each regional group. Panel B reflects CIT incentives registered in the OECD ITID with at least one eligibility condition. The number of incentives that have specific eligibility criteria is 69 (ECOWAS) and 395 (Other developing economies). Shares do not add up to 100% because incentives can have multiple eligibility criteria.
Source: OECD ITID, April 2023, based on 52 economies and 464 CIT incentive entries.

Overall, many incentives in ECOWAS are fairly broadly targeted, available to investors in many sectors and regions. Location-based incentives tend to be available for investors in most parts of the country. In some cases, the set of eligible recipients is limited to large investors, but minimum investment thresholds can also cast a wide net. When large segments of the economy are eligible for incentives, it is harder to monitor uptake and compliance, and to evaluate if incentives are benefiting firms or activities that would not develop without the incentive.

In some cases, broad targeting (for example of sectors) can ease distortions to competition. The EU, for example, prohibits narrow sector targeting of incentives geared to support regional development to promote fair competition (under EU State Aid rules). Incentives are by their nature distortionary, and therefore should ideally be limited to address market failures, which tend to be more specific than the scope of sectors and activities eligible for incentives in ECOWAS, and indeed most countries covered by the database. Broad targeting also raises questions as to the extent to which incentives are used instead of wider tax policy reform. Incentives are costly for public finances, and will necessitate lower public spending, higher debt, or higher taxes elsewhere. Broad incentives may cost similar amounts of revenue compared to reductions in standard tax rates, which may be less complex to administer and comply with. Incentives are not effective as a replacement to other policies to improve the investment climate, including good governance (OECD, 2015[33]).

Sector-based eligibility conditions are widely used

All of the seven ECOWAS Member States covered offer incentives conditional on sector of activity. Most of these define eligible sectors in a positive list (the focus of this section), although some carve out certain activities as eligible to benefit from the incentive, for example, mining and extraction. Sector targeting can be broad (e.g. the incentive is available to investors active in all sub-sectors within a sector, e.g. the entire manufacturing or agricultural sector) or narrow (only available to a specific set of sub-sectors (e.g. a tax exemption for automobile manufacturers in Ghana).

Most sector-based incentives in the selected ECOWAS countries support investors in agriculture (41% of all incentives), followed by manufacturing (36%) and services (32%) (Figure 4.4). This means that incentives are available to investors operating in these broad sector categories or in a subset of industries. The only sub-sector supported by every country is crops and animals. For manufacturing, the sub-industries most frequently supported by incentives are food and beverage, textile and apparel, rubber and non-minerals, metals, and motor vehicles. All of the selected ECOWAS Member States offer some incentives for service sectors, though far fewer incentives (as a percentage of the total incentives offered) target services compared to ASEAN countries. Service sub-sectors most often supported in ECOWAS are tourism, ICT, finance and real estate, and construction.

Around a quarter of sector-based incentives in the ECOWAS Member States target extractive industries (including coal, oil and gas, metal ore and other mining). Of the seven countries covered, only Côte d'Ivoire does not offer incentives for extraction as it recently repealed a five-year tax exemption for income from mining activities. Most incentives are accelerated allowances to support high initial capital costs, but some countries provide full CIT exemptions for petroleum refineries (Sierra Leone), solid mineral mining (Nigeria), and petroleum exploration and mining of precious stones (Gambia). While incentives during exploration periods and other taxes including royalty rates are often important for investors in extractive industries, full CIT incentives for mining generally appear to be both ineffective at attracting additional investment, and inefficient (i.e., costs are greater than benefits). Because extractive industries are location-specific, incentives are less likely to sway investment location decisions. Mining investors are not as easily able to relocate to other jurisdictions with greater tax benefits than more mobile investors less tied to the location (IGF-OECD, 2018[34]; James, 2014[7]). CIT exemptions then bring substantial rents to companies that may have invested even without the incentive.

Just under half of the incentives with sector-related criteria target multiple sector categories (e.g. agriculture and manufacturing) at once, usually two or three. Most of these incentives have other eligibility criteria, including investment in a particular location or economic zone (which might accept a variety of industries), or a minimum investment value. Several incentives are available to broadly defined priority sectors, with other conditions to benefit. For example, in Nigeria the government sets a list of "pioneer industries"; companies in these sectors with large-scale investment plans can apply to receive CIT exemptions. By comparison, ASEAN countries also grant most sector-based incentives to investors in multiple sector categories, while the LAC countries covered in the database mostly target their sector incentives to just one sector (e.g. only the manufacturing sector or manufacturing sub-sectors). Narrower sector targeting can be a means to contain costs of incentives by focusing only on sectors or sub-sectors considered most likely in need of support or able to create social and economic spillovers (Celani, Dressler and Wermelinger, 2022[1]).

Figure 4.4. Sector-based incentives favour agriculture, manufacturing and services

% of incentives registered in the OECD ITID

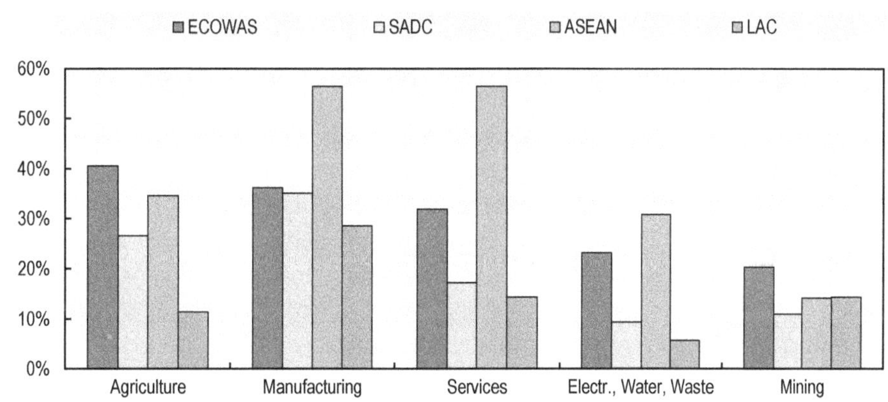

Note: See Box 4.1 for information on countries covered in each regional group. The number of registered incentives in each region is: 128 (SADC), 69 (ECOWAS), 78 (ASEAN), 19 (EaP), 35 (LAC). Incentives can be specific to one or more sub-sectors within these five sector categories, or are available to any investor that falls under the broad category. Shares do not add up to 100% as incentives can target multiple sectors.

Source: OECD ITID April 2023, based on 52 economies and 464 CIT incentive entries.

Investment location and size are also key conditions

Investment location is the next most frequently used eligibility criteria among the selected ECOWAS economies, including requirements related to specific geographic regions (in six out of seven countries) or special economic zones (in five out of seven countries). Among ECOWAS Member States examined, every country but Sierra Leone incentivises investments in designated locations, often to promote investment in under-developed areas. For example, Nigeria provides a tax allowance for capital expenditure on infrastructure facilities (water, electricity) for businesses in rural areas (defined as areas located more than 20km away from government-supplied infrastructure). Several location-based tax incentives are available to eligible investors that locate anywhere outside of the capital city, for example in Côte d'Ivoire and Senegal.

A minimum investment size requirement is used in four out of the seven ECOWAS Member States. Most incentives in ECOWAS that target by investment size require firms to meet both a minimum investment value and employment requirement (overall job creation or commitment to hire a certain number or percentage of nationals). Other regions covered in the database also tend to link minimum investment value to employment requirements, though in the SADC, EaP and ASEAN countries covered fewer countries use investment value requirements combined with employment outcome conditions. Some ECOWAS countries link minimum investment requirements to most of their CIT exemptions (Gambia and Sierra Leone). This could be a means to tie the benefit – which as noted earlier is unrelated to the amount of capital invested – to physical presence in the country. While such criteria can ensure a minimum expenditure in the host country, they require administrative resources to monitor if the criterion was met. However, the other risks associated with CIT exemptions persist (James, 2014[7]).

Outcome conditions focus on export promotion and employment

Outcome-related criteria require companies to achieve certain performance results to be eligible for a tax incentive. They are linked to the outcome of the investment, rather than the characteristics of the qualifying investor (Celani, Dressler and Wermelinger, 2022[1]). For example, around half of the ECOWAS Member States considered offer at least one incentive that requires a minimum share of exports in total sales. Many incentives in the region are also linked to job creation, either through a requirement that the firm must employ a specific number of national (or overall) employees, or less precise commitments to contribute to job creation.

Outcome conditions can be designed to promote positive social and environmental spillovers or other economic goals. For example, in Eswatini, investors in SEZs are required to pay wages that are 90% above the minimum wage to receive a tax exemption. South Africa granted a tax allowance on machinery and training costs if the project meets a combination of (mostly) quantifiable criteria related to energy efficiency, innovation, SME procurement and local linkages.[4] Several countries in ASEAN and SADC, offer incentives conditional on a certain share of domestic value added to firm output or revenue. In the ECOWAS, as across other regions, outcome conditions are most often used for CIT exemptions. This may be an effort to improve the design of these instruments, perhaps reducing the risk that footloose investors use tax exemptions without contributing to economic substance in the country. However, often outcome conditions are vague or based on non-quantifiable criteria (e.g., contributes to job creation or beneficial to the national economy), leaving ample room for discretionary approval of incentives by awarding authorities. Performance criteria also require monitoring to ensure that the outcome has been met, which requires public resources, administrative capacity, and often coordination with other government agencies (e.g., cross-checking with social security information on number of jobs created or salary).

Many incentives designed to support economic and other development goals

Many countries use investment incentives in an effort to advance certain economic, social, environmental and other goals. As noted, this can be through incentive eligibility conditions that require investors to meet certain performance criteria (e.g. job creation) or operate in certain sectors (e.g. renewable energy), or by designing the incentive to reduce the costs of certain activities (e.g. R&D, training), and increasing the revenues associated with others (e.g. exports). While incentives have the potential to contribute to these goals, the costs of administering and monitoring compliance with stated performance criteria can be high. Furthermore, tax policy or other types of incentives (such as grants or in-kind subsidies) are not the only way to encourage the industrial development or influence investor behaviour, and tax incentives should at most be complementary to other policy tools (OECD, 2022[26]).

Based on analysis on design features and eligibility conditions of incentives in the selected ECOWAS Member States, the main goals of incentives offered are to encourage infrastructure development (supported by 25% of incentives, used in all seven countries), employment and job creation (22%, in five countries), and exports (14%, in four countries) (Figure 4.5, Panel A). Other goals include promoting the green transition (supported by 13% of incentives, used in six countries) and extraction of natural resources (13%, in five countries), while few seek to improve working conditions and skills (3%, in Côte d'Ivoire and Ghana) or advance social inclusion (1%, in Côte d'Ivoire), and there are no incentives that promote linkages with the local economy. Some ECOWAS countries also have incentives to support innovation or research and development, which is not illustrated in the figure. In contrast to SADC and other regions, ECOWAS Member States use incentives more often to support job creation and infrastructure.

These findings show that most of the seven ECOWAS Member States tie at least some of their incentives to sustainable development aims (Figure 4.5, Panel B). However, this does not necessarily mean that incentives are designed foremost to support those aims, or that they are either successful or the most effective way to do so. For example, employment requirements can be a means to limit tax benefits to only large firms. These firms might create more jobs but might not need the fiscal incentive in order to do so, creating windfall profits for firms that already have market power at the expense of government revenue forgone and potentially fair competition.

Conversely, more targeted incentives could encourage types of employment that might not occur otherwise. Several countries in the region provide examples: Ghana offers an enhanced deduction for salaries of recent Ghanian graduates of tertiary institutions. Côte d'Ivoire offers tax credits for hiring nationals with a proven handicap, and for new hires in non-fixed term contracts. Fiscal benefits could also incentivise firms to undertake activities they might not otherwise do, such as training and R&D. Nigeria offers an allowance for any organisation engaged in R&D for commercialisation, and the Gambia has a reduced CIT rate for domestic firms in technology or R&D that (among other conditions) have a skills development programme to train Gambians in the IT field. Monitoring and evaluation are key to assess if these incentives support stated goals, and at what costs (including administration costs). Higher administrative costs for implementing more targeted incentives may also be a reason why these types of incentive are less prevalent in the region.

Figure 4.5. Many incentives in ECOWAS support development goals

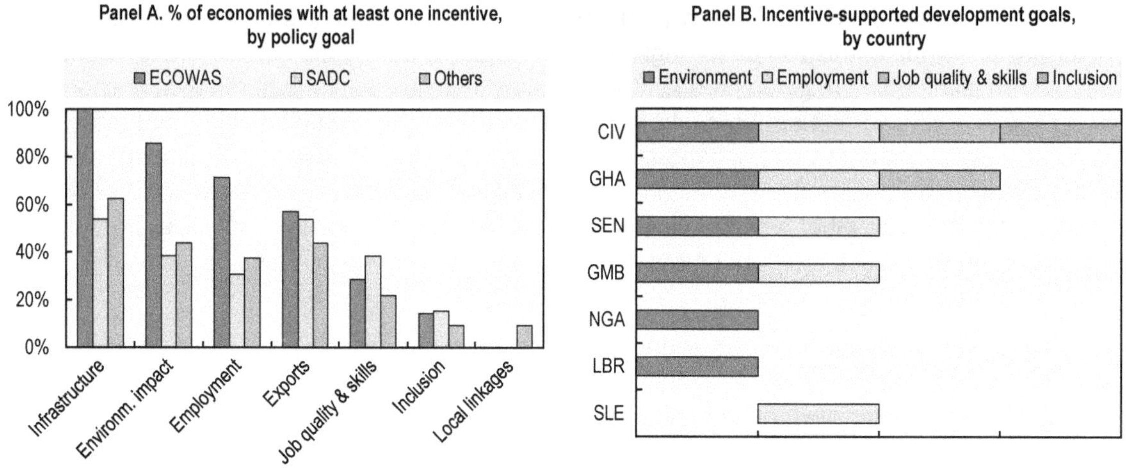

Note: See Box 4.1 for information on countries covered in reach regional group and Annex A for indicator methodology. The total number of incentives in each region is: 69 (ECOWAS), 128 (SADC), and 267 (other developing regions). Panel B indicates that countries support respective development goals with at least one CIT incentive.
Source: OECD ITID April 2023, based on 52 economies and 464 CIT incentive entries.

Incentive governance is split between Ministry of Finance and IPA

Governance of incentives includes how tax benefits are authorised in laws or regulations and awarded to investors. It also concerns whether incentives are transparent, and whether eligibility conditions to receive incentives are clear and specific, or based on interpretation and approval from administering authorities. Governance also involves how compliance with incentive conditions is monitored and incentive policies evaluated ex-post.

All ECOWAS Member States under consideration grant tax incentives through the Ministry of Finance, although some Member States grant incentives also through Investment Promotion Agencies or other governmental bodies (Figure 4.6). The Ministry of Finance is often best placed to grant incentives and monitor their costs. Other ministries or agencies may be more inclined to offer fiscal benefits as they are not in charge of tax collection or necessarily aware of the state's fiscal needs (James, 2014[7]). Besides Gambia, all ECOWAS countries examined introduce incentives in the tax law (64% of registered incentives), although some countries also use other legislation, such as investment laws (8%), SEZ laws (7%) or regulations (4%). There is broad international consensus that consolidating all tax incentives in tax laws enhances transparency and reduces potential redundancies and confusion over the administering authority (IMF-OECD-UN-World Bank, 2015[12]).

Similar to other regions, almost all countries covered in the database (except Sierra Leone) also grant some incentives through other government agencies, most often the investment promotion agencies (IPAs), other ministries (e.g. ministry of investment or industry), and SEZ authorities. In four ECOWAS countries, different agencies share responsibility for granting at least one incentive. Different agencies can bring valuable insights for incentive design, monitoring and evaluation. But without effective coordination incentives may overlap, be inconsistent, or work at cross-purposes (IMF-OECD-UN-World Bank, 2015[12]). Administration of incentives by multiple authorities with overlapping responsibilities, can also increase opportunities for aggressive tax planning by investors.

Figure 4.6. ECOWAS countries grant tax incentives through the Ministry of Finance but some countries grant incentives also through IPAs and other government bodies

% of economies with at least one CIT incentive per governing authority

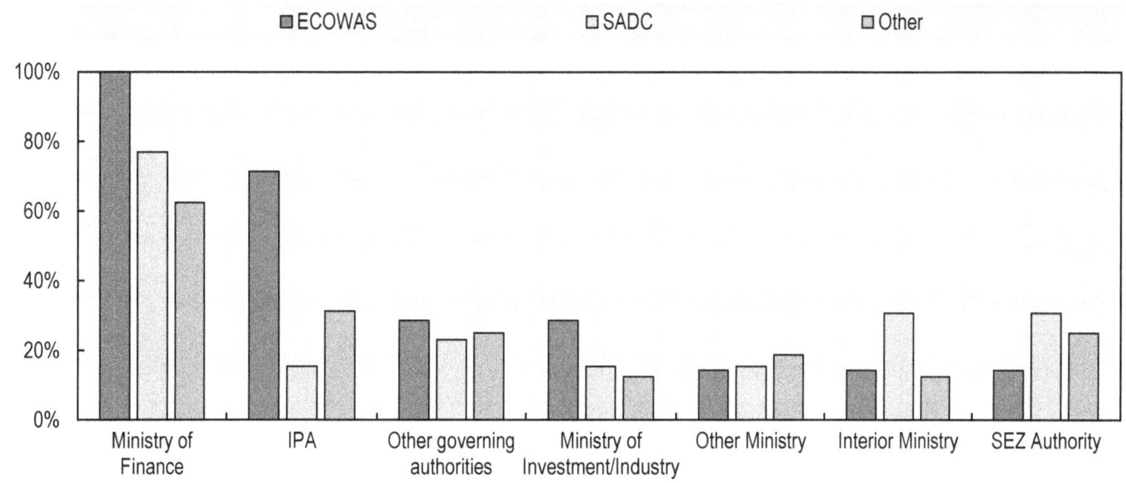

Note: See Box 4.1 for information on countries covered in reach regional group. The number of incentives for which the details of granting authorities are available in each region is 63 (ECOWAS); 107 (SADC); 250 (Other).
Source: OECD ITID, April 2023, based on 52 economies and 464 CIT incentive entries.

Most CIT incentives in the selected ECOWAS Member States are transparent, in that eligibility criteria to receive the benefit are clearly stated in laws and regulations and tend to be specific (e.g. lists of eligible sectors). However, as in other regions, in some instances, qualifying expenditure eligible for tax allowances and credits is vague, leaving room for interpretation or confusion. Moreover, there are some incentives that are less transparent due to vaguely defined eligibility criteria (e.g. contributing to economic development and job creation), and in some cases investors are eligible for additional tax benefits not specified in laws.

When granting authorities have wide discretion to determine who can receive incentives and the extent of benefits, it increases the risk of rent-seeking behaviour and corruption, as well as unfair competition between firms (IMF-OECD-UN-World Bank, 2015[12]). The OECD ITID also only covers CIT incentives introduced in legal texts, many countries grant incentives on an ad hoc negotiated basis with investors (e.g., through bilateral contracts); these are by their nature non-transparent. Further analysis is required to assess governance across the full life cycle of the incentive, including monitoring and evaluation.

Assessing the impact of incentives: next steps

For governments, better understanding of whether incentives contribute to policy goals, and at what costs, requires comprehensive monitoring and evaluation (M&E), although this requires data and resources that are often not available. Short of more in-depth cost-benefit analysis, governments can do more to track incentive goals and use. An important first step to create accountability and transparency is identifying and describing all available incentives, their policy goal, and legal reference in publicly available documents. This is particularly important if different agencies are involved in granting incentives. Governments can regularly assess if stated goals of tax incentives, align with investment promotion strategies and national development goals (Chapter 3).

As a next step, information on incentive uptake and characteristics of beneficiary firms can provide important insights into how incentives are used, and if incentives appear to be supporting projects most in need. Many ECOWAS Member States, as in other regions, require that firms apply to receive benefits. Though this can introduce a risk of discretionary awarding of incentives, if based on clear and specific eligibility criteria, incentive applications could form the basis of initial monitoring. More in-depth monitoring of firm compliance with the terms of the incentive (for example, jobs created, value of exports), can assist in determining if the incentive is contributing to development goals.

To compare how these benefits measure against costs, tax expenditure reports are key to estimate revenue forgone. However, challenges to tax expenditure reporting include the type of data the tax authorities collect, lack of coordination across agencies involved in granting tax incentives, data that is not yet digitised, and challenges with both data and human resources in the Ministry of Finance (ATI-CEP-IDOS, 2022[35]). In addition, some incentives are by their nature more difficult to monitor. Beneficiaries of tax exemptions may not have to file tax returns, complicating assessments of costs in terms of revenues forgone (Klemm, 2009[36]).

Some countries in ECOWAS are conducting tax expenditure reporting and have put in place dedicated teams to conduct fiscal evaluation (ECOWAS-UEMOA, 2022[6]). Some countries have also conducted specific evaluations. With support from a private analytical firm, the government of Côte d'Ivoire estimated the impact of a five-year CIT exemption for a gold mine, finding that the mine was profitable even without fiscal benefits, and the substantial loss in forgone revenue was not justified (IGF-OECD, 2018[34]). Côte d'Ivoire repealed its CIT exemptions for mining in 2020.

However, according to a recent ECOWAS report, no study yet includes any social or economic effects of incentives, and expenditure reports seem to be intended as much to justify continued use of incentives as to study their costs (ECOWAS-UEMOA, 2022[6]). These reports are also often not published or drafted to be made accessible to by a wider audience. Of particular interest for future analysis is how tax incentives affect the effective tax rates of firms – a first step towards evaluating costs of incentives – and which incentives appear most effective at promoting positive development outcomes, beyond investment attraction.

ECOWAS could play an important role in supporting incentive monitoring and evaluation, as well as to promote transparency and good governance in incentive policies. The ECOWAS Secretariat has engaged in efforts to support tax expenditure reporting in member states. (One such programme, West African Tax Transition Support Programme (PAFT), funded by the EU, provides capacity building on evaluation of tax expenditure, focuses mostly on VAT). As part of this, there have been calls to develop a harmonised regional framework for assessing tax expenditures across ECOWAS, including economic and social effects of tax incentives (not just revenue forgone). This would also allow for comparisons across countries based on a common methodology (ECOWAS-UEMOA, 2022[6]).

Greater coordination at the regional level on tax incentive use could help reduce tax competition, promote evaluation of costly policies, and provide guidelines for good governance and transparency. Article 23 of the Supplementary Act to the ECOWAS Treaty Adopting Community Rules on Investment suggests that Member States avoid competition for the attraction of investments through incentives or other means that distort regional competition for investments. Furthermore, the ECOWAS Investment Policy notes that "the relatively aggressive use of financial and non-financial incentives to attract investment in the region has often induced unhealthy competition amongst the Member States. The lack of harmonisation or, at least, overall consistency in investment-incentives schemes across the common market has adversely affected, at times, the regional investment climate. Another negative outcome of so-called 'race to the bottom' tendencies is the heightened economic and social costs that are attributable to forgone national government tax revenue." (ECOWAS Commission, 2018[37]).

Notes

[1] Forward-looking corporate effective tax rates (ETRs) are a way of measuring the extent to which tax incentives affect tax costs and influence business investment and location decisions. Forward-looking ETRs are a useful indicator to compare the impact of tax incentives on effective taxation. The composite Effective Average Tax Rate (EATR) is constructed as a weighted average across finance- and asset-specific EATRs. It is a synthetic tax policy indicator reflecting the average tax contribution a firm makes on an investment project earning above-zero economic profits over its lifetime. The EATR is a useful indicator to compare the generosity of distinct types of preferential tax treatment relative to the standard tax treatment and to assess tax relief from investing in one as opposed to another sector, region or country or to assess the relief provided through specific incentive designs everything else being equal.

[2] Data from the Global Tax Expenditures Database (GTED) and OECD revenue statistics. Available data from the GTED also suggest that in several ECOWAS Member States other tax incentives, including VAT and excise taxes (on fuel for example), cost more in revenue forgone than incentives on CIT or other taxes on income (Redonda, von Haldenwang and Aliu, 2022[21]). In ECOWAS, VAT harmonisation has been a particular challenge (IMF, 2021[19]). This shows the importance of looking at the full scope of tax benefits available for investors in considering both the costs of incentives and their policy goals, and would merit further research and analysis. The GTED data covers 18 jurisdictions in Africa, 12 jurisdictions in Asia-Pacific, 33 jurisdictions in Europe and North America and 14 jurisdictions in the LAC region. OECD Revenue Statistics cover 29 jurisdictions in Africa, 23 in Asia-Pacific, 32 in Europe and North America and 26 jurisdictions in LAC.

[3] The definition of permanent here refers to incentives that do not limit by design the period of the preferential treatment even if sunset clauses apply to the legal basis. Sunset clauses may apply to both temporary and permanent incentives. The definition of temporary here refers to incentives that provide preferential treatment over a limited period in time by design, i.e. a specific period in which a tax exemption or reduced rate applies. It does not make a reference to the temporary nature of the incentive's legal basis, e.g. in cases where sunset clauses apply.

[4] This tax allowance in South Africa was introduced in the Income Tax Act, Section 12I, and got repealed in March 2020.

References

Abbas, S. and A. Klemm (2013), "A partial race to the bottom: Corporate tax developments in emerging and developing economies", *International Tax and Public Finance*, Vol. 20/4, pp. 596-617, https://doi.org/10.1007/S10797-013-9286-8/TABLES/5. [15]

Abramovsky, L. et al. (2018), "Are corporate tax incentives for investment fit for purpose? Revisiting economic principles and evidence from low- and middle-income countries", https://doi.org/10.1920/RE.IFS.2018.0142. [29]

Andersen, M., B. Kett and E. von Uexkull (2018), "Corporate Tax Incentives and FDI in Developing Countries", in *Global Investment Competitiveness Report 2017/2018: Foreign Investor Perspectives and Policy Implications*, World Bank Group, Washington, DC, https://pubdocs.worldbank.org/en/964321508856694021/GICR-03.pdf (accessed on [8]

11 May 2021).

Appelt, S., A. González Cabral and T. Hanappi (2022), "Income-based tax incentives for R&D and innovation: Measures of tax expenditure and uptake", *OECD Science, Technology and Innovation Working Paper series*, OECD, Paris. [24]

ATI-CEP-IDOS (2022), *Workshop Report*, Addis Tax Initiative (ATI), Council on Economic Policies (CEP), German Institute of Development and Sustainability (IDOS), https://www.addistaxinitiative.net/sites/default/files/resources/Report-ATI%20Regional%20Workshop%20%28En%29.pdf (accessed on 5 March 2023). [35]

Celani, A., L. Dressler and T. Hanappi (2022), "Assessing tax relief from targeted investment tax incentives through corporate effective tax rates", *OECD Taxation Working Paper Series*, OECD, Paris, https://doi.org/10.1787/22235558. [18]

Celani, A., L. Dressler and M. Wermelinger (2022), "OECD Investment Tax Incentives Database: Enhancing transparency through comparable data in developing countries", *OECD Working Papers on International Investment*, OECD, Paris, https://doi.org/10.1787/62e075a9-en. [1]

Chai, J. and R. Goyal (2008), "Tax Concessions and Foreign Direct Investment in the Eastern Caribbean Currency Union", *IMF Working Papers*, No. 2008/257, International Monetary Fund, https://www.imf.org/en/Publications/WP/Issues/2016/12/31/Tax-Concessions-and-Foreign-Direct-Investment-in-the-Eastern-Caribbean-Currency-Union-22456. [13]

ECOWAS Commission (2018), *ECOWAS Investment Policy*, https://wacomp.projects.ecowas.int/wp-content/uploads/2020/03/ECOWAS-INVESTMENT-POLICY-ENGLISH.pdf. [37]

ECOWAS-UEMOA (2022), *Guide méthodologique d'évaluation régionale des dépenses fiscales en Afrique de l'Ouest*, ECOWAS, UEMOA, Programme d'Appui à la Transition Fiscale (PATF), https://www.patf-ao.org/wp-content/uploads/2022/07/GUIDE-METHODOLOGIQUE-DEVALUATION-DES-DEPENSES-FISCALES-EN-AFRIQUE-DE-LOUEST_VERSION-DU-28-Juillet-2022.pdf (accessed on 5 March 2023). [6]

Ghrara, S. and B. El Morchid (2022), "Congés fiscaux et afflux des IDE dans les pays de la CEDEAO : Une application à l'aide de l'approche PMG", *International Journal of Accounting, Finance, Auditing, Management and Economics*, Vol. 3/4-1, pp. 21-42, https://doi.org/10.5281/ZENODO.6612018. [9]

House, C. and M. Shapiro (2008), "Temporary Investment Tax Incentives: Theory with Evidence from Bonus Depreciation", *American Economic Review*, Vol. 98/3, pp. 737-768, https://doi.org/10.1257/aer.98.3.737. [23]

IGF-OECD (2018), *Tax Incentives in Mining: Minimising risks to revenue*, Intergovernmental Forum on Mining, Minerals, Metals and Sustainable Development (IGF) and OECD, https://www.oecd.org/tax/beps/tax-incentives-in-mining-minimising-risks-to-revenue-oecd-igf.pdf (accessed on 8 March 2023). [34]

IMF (2021), "West African Economic and Monetary Union: Staff Report on Common Policies for Member Countries-Press Release; Staff Report; and Statement by the Executive Director for the West African Economic and Monetary Union", *Country Report*, [19]

No. 2021/049, IMF, Washington, DC, https://www.imf.org/en/Publications/CR/Issues/2021/03/02/West-African-Economic-and-Monetary-Union-Staff-Report-on-Common-Policies-for-Member-50139 (accessed on 5 March 2023).

IMF, OECD, UN, World Bank (2015), *Options for Low Income Countries' Effective and Efficient Use of Ta Incentives for Investment, A report to the G-20 Development Working Group*, https://www.imf.org/external/np/g20/pdf/101515.pdf. [25]

IMF-OECD (2017), *Tax Certainty: IMF/OECD Report for the G20 Finance Ministers*, IMF and OECD, https://www.oecd.org/tax/tax-policy/tax-certainty-report-oecd-imf-report-g20-finance-ministers-march-2017.pdf. [11]

IMF-OECD-UN-World Bank (2015), *Options for Low Income Countries' Effective and Efficient Use of Tax Incentives for Investment*, A report prepared for the G-20 Development Working Group by the IMF, OECD, UN and World Bank., https://www.oecd.org/tax/options-for-low-income-countries-effective-and-efficient-use-of-tax-incentives-for-investment.htm. [12]

James, S. (2014), *Tax and Non-Tax Incentives and Investments: Evidence and Policy Implications*, World Bank, Washington DC, https://papers.ssrn.com/sol3/papers.cfm?abstract_id=2401905. [7]

Keen, M. and M. Mansour (2009), "Revenue Mobilization in Sub-Saharan Africa: Challenges from Globalization", *IMF Working Papers*, No. 157, IMF, Washington, DC, https://www.imf.org/external/pubs/ft/wp/2009/wp09157.pdf (accessed on 17 March 2023). [14]

Klemm, A. (2009), "Causes, Benefits, and Risks of Business Tax Incentives", *IMF Working Paper*, No. 2009/021, IMF, Washington, DC, https://www.imf.org/en/Publications/WP/Issues/2016/12/31/Causes-Benefits-and-Risks-of-Business-Tax-Incentives-22628 (accessed on 1 March 2023). [36]

Klemm, A. and S. Van Parys (2012), "Empirical evidence on the effects of tax incentives", *International Tax and Public Finance*, Vol. 19/3, pp. 393-423, https://doi.org/10.1007/S10797-011-9194-8/METRICS. [4]

Lent, G. (1967), "Tax Incentives for Investment in Developing Countries", *IMF Staff Papers*, Vol. 1967/002, https://doi.org/10.5089/9781451947250.024.A003. [30]

Morisset, J. and N. Pirnia (1999), "How Tax Policy and Incentives Affect Foreign Direct Investment: A Review", *Foreign Investment Advisory Service*, World Bank, Washington, D.C., https://papers.ssrn.com/sol3/papers.cfm?abstract_id=632579 (accessed on 9 March 2023). [28]

OECD (2023), *Corporate TAx Statistics Database*, https://stats.oecd.org/Index.aspx?DataSetCode=CTS_CIT. [16]

OECD (2022), *FDI Qualities Indicators 2022*, https://www.oecd.org/investment/investment-policy/OECD-FDI-Qualities-Indicators-2022-update.pdf. [38]

OECD (2022), *FDI Qualities Policy Toolkit*, OECD Publishing, Paris, https://doi.org/10.1787/7ba74100-en. [26]

OECD (2022), *FDI Qualities Policy Toolkit*, OECD Publishing, Paris, https://doi.org/10.1787/7ba74100-en. [39]

OECD (2022), *OECD Investment Tax Incentives Database – 2022 Update: Tax incentives for sustainable development (brochure)*, OECD, Paris, http://www.oecd.org/investment/investment-policy/oecdinvestment-tax-incentives-database-2022-update-brochure.pdf (accessed on 14 March 2023). [2]

OECD (2022), *Tax Incentives and the Global Minimum Corporate Tax: Reconsidering Tax Incentives after the GloBE Rules*, OECD Publishing, Paris, https://doi.org/10.1787/25d30b96-en. [20]

OECD (2015), *Policy Framework for Investment, 2015 Edition*, OECD Publishing, Paris, https://doi.org/10.1787/9789264208667-en. [33]

PwC (2020), *Paying Taxes 2020: data explorer*, Paying Taxes 2020, https://www.pwc.com/gx/en/services/tax/publications/paying-taxes-2020/explorer-tool.html (accessed on 5 March 2023). [5]

Redonda, A., C. von Haldenwang and F. Aliu (2022), *Global Tax Expenditures Database [data set], Version 1.1.4*. [21]

Tax Foundation (2022), *Corporate Tax Rates around the World, 2022*, https://taxfoundation.org/data/all/global/corporate-tax-rates-by-country-2022/. [17]

UN-CIAT (2018), *Design and Assessment of Tax Incentives in Developing Countries: Selected Issues and a Country Experience*, United Nations, Inter-American Center of Tax Administrations, https://www.un.org/esa/ffd/wp-content/uploads/2018/02/tax-incentives_eng.pdf (accessed on 9 March 2023). [27]

UNIDO (2013), *Africa Investor Survey*, United Nations Industrial Development Organization. [10]

US Department of the Treasury (2010), *The Case for Temporary 100 Percent Expensing: Encouraging Business to Expand Now By Lowering the Cost of Investment*, US Department of the Treasury Office of Tax Policy, Washington, DC, https://home.treasury.gov/system/files/131/Report-Temporary-100percent-Expensing-2010.pdf (accessed on 1 March 2023). [32]

Van Parys, S. and S. James (2010), "The effectiveness of tax incentives in attracting investment: panel data evidence from the CFA Franc zone", *International Tax and Public Finance*, Vol. 17/4, pp. 400-429, https://doi.org/10.1007/s10797-010-9140-1. [3]

Wen, J. (2020), *IMF Fiscal Affairs Special Series on COVID-19: Temporary Investment Incentives*, IMF, Washington, DC, https://www.imf.org/en/Publications/SPROLLs/covid19-special-notes (accessed on 1 March 2023). [31]

Zee, H., J. Stotsky and E. Ley (2002), "Tax Incentives for Business Investment: A Primer for Policy Makers in Developing Countries", *World Development*, Vol. 30/9, pp. 1497-1516, https://doi.org/10.1016/S0305-750X(02)00050-5. [22]

Annex A. Additional details on classifications

The ITID considers policy area being targeted by evaluating whether a specific design or eligibility condition of the tax incentive relates to one of six policy goals (Table 1). The policy areas identified in the ITID build on those identified in the OECD FDI Qualities Indicators (OECD, 2022[38]) and the FDI Qualities policy toolkit (OECD, 2022[39]).

Table 1. Targeting sustainable development through eligibility conditions and design dimensions of investment tax incentives

Column 1 lists policy areas identified in the ITID. The table identifies how economies target these respective clusters, either through eligibility conditions or the design features of tax incentives (columns 2-5).

(1) Sustainable Development Areas	(2) Outcome condition	(3) Sector condition	(4) Preferential treatment for certain qualifying income	(5) Preferential treatment for certain qualifying expenditure
Employment & job creation	(a) Create a minimum number of new jobs;			(a) Wages of newly created jobs; (b) Wages of recent graduates; (c) Wages of employees, including for women or workers with disabilities.
Environmental impact	(a) Ensure some or a certain level of energy efficiency improvement.	(a) Electricity generation from renewable energy sources;[1] (b) Waste management.		(a) Acquisition of machinery for electricity production from renewable energy sources; (b) Improving the energy performance of machinery or buildings (e.g. via building retrofitting).
Job quality and skills	(a) Reach a minimum level of expenditure on training and education; (b) Pay an average wage at a certain level.			(a) Expenditure on training and education of employees; (b) Wages of trainees and apprentices; (c) Training expenditures for women re-entering the workforce or workers with disabilities; (d) Expenditures related to building training facilities.
Local linkages	(a) Source a minimum share of inputs from the local market; (b) Source a minimum share of inputs from local SMEs.			(a) Expenditures on inputs sourced from SMEs.
Promoting Exports	(a) Achieve a minimum export share in sales.		(a) Income from exports; (b) Income from transit trade.	(a) Export promotion expenditure.[2]
Social Inclusion	(a) Employ a minimum share of female workers;			(a) Wages of female workers or workers with disabilities;

	(b) Employ a minimum share of workers with disabilities; (c) Founding members of a company must be people with disabilities.			(b) Training expenditures for women re-entering the workforce or workers with disabilities.

Notes: Eligibility conditions and design features listed in the table are used by at least one economy included in the database. The list may evolve in the future when economy coverage extends.
[1] Includes only tax incentives benefiting electricity generation from renewable energy sources, but not electricity generation from non-renewable sources. Tax incentive may be part of a broader special regime that benefits other sector of the economy.
[2] Refers to expenses incurred for the purpose of seeking opportunities and promoting the export of goods or services produced in the economy (e.g. publicity and advertisements abroad, export market research, participation in trade fairs amongst others).

Other policy goals commonly targeted with tax incentives relate to infrastructure and innovation. Infrastructure can relate to a broad set of areas, including transport, utilities (e.g. electricity or gas distribution, water and sewage disposal structures), construction or ICT. CIT incentives promoting innovation commonly target R&D-related costs (e.g. wages of R&D employees, current costs of R&D projects, assets) or income (e.g. income from R&D or registered patents).

5 Promoting investment for green growth

Foreign direct investment (FDI) can contribute the needed financial and technological resources to deliver green growth. This chapter discusses the specific enabling conditions for green investment in ECOWAS, including key elements of the broader framework for environmental protection, and policies designed to attract and facilitate green FDI.

Investment for green growth needs to be scaled-up significantly to advance sustainable development in West Africa, and achieve national economic, social and environmental policy goals. Green growth means fostering growth and development while preserving natural assets, and ensuring that they continue to provide the resources and environmental services on which our well-being relies. Beyond minimising the environmental footprint of investments in general, this requires investments in new technologies, services and infrastructure that make more sustainable claims on natural resources (green investments). Under certain circumstances, foreign direct investment (FDI) can contribute the needed financial and technological resources to deliver green growth. But foreign investors can also deteriorate environmental outcomes and hamper sustainable development. This chapter discusses the specific enabling conditions for green investment in ECOWAS, including key elements of the broader framework for environmental protection, and policies designed to attract and facilitate green FDI.

Green growth and climate change in West Africa

The Economic Community of West African States (ECOWAS) faces both challenges and opportunities in its path toward green growth. Challenges include a heavy dependence on natural resources and unsustainable use of these resulting in degradation of land and water, a major investment gap for basic infrastructure and increasing vulnerability to climate change and extreme weather. Addressing these challenges also presents an opportunity for ECOWAS to promote green investment. The imperative to urgently scale up access to electricity and promote energy security, the region's high renewable energy potential and the need to improve the efficiency of how natural resources are used illustrate the potential for green investment in West Africa. A measured and inclusive approach, based on a sound policy framework that promotes investment in green sectors and facilitates the greening of investment overall, can help address challenges and promote sustainable development in ECOWAS.

Natural resources are critical for continued development in West Africa

West African countries are at different stages of development, but almost all their economies, have grown by over 80%, and twelve have more than doubled since 2000 (Table 5.1). ECOWAS countries have relied heavily on natural resources to support economic development in past decades, and primary sectors continue to contribute substantially, despite the rising importance of services, and to a lesser extent, industry. In 2020, agriculture, forestry and fishing made up over 20% of GDP in 10 Member States, with Sierra Leone (60%), Liberia (41%), Niger (38%) and Mali (36%) depending disproportionately on subsistence agriculture. Rents from natural resources amounted to over 9% of GDP in six ECOWAS countries, with forestry rents in excess of 10% in Liberia (15%) and Guinea-Bissau (11%), and coal rents amounting to 11% of Cabo Verde's GDP.

Heavy reliance on natural resources for development, coupled with unstainable use of these resources, means that the environment costs of growth have been high. Forest cover in the region has shrunk by 19% over the last thirty years, compared to a 15% decrease in Africa as a whole, a 4% decrease in non-OECD countries and a 2% increase in forest cover in the OECD (Figure 5.1). All but two ECOWAS countries (Cabo Verde and Mali) have seen their forests shrink, with the largest drops observed in Côte d'Ivoire (65%), the Gambia (41%) and Benin (35%). In some countries, desertification and high population growth are putting pressures on the few remaining forest lands.

Deforestation and land degradation have also been major drivers of biodiversity loss and rising carbon emissions. While West Africa is responsible for less than 1% of global CO_2 emissions, and 13% of Africa's emissions, emissions per unit of GDP have risen in all but three ECOWAS economies, by 20% on average since 2000 (Figure 5.2). This is contrast with declining carbon emissions per unit of output in Africa as a whole and non-OECD countries more generally. Urbanisation has exacerbated land degradation and biodiversity loss and brought additional environmental challenges. According to the 2022 Environmental

Performance Index that covers 180 countries worldwide, most ECOWAS countries rank poorly in terms of progress toward improving environmental health, protecting ecosystems, and mitigating climate change, with eleven countries ranking among the lowest 50 scores (Wolf et al., 2022[1]).

Table 5.1. Selected economic and environmental indicators

MS	GDP growth over 2000-2021 (%)	Agriculture, forestry & fishing (% of GDP)	Natural resource rents (% of GDP)	Rural population (% of population)	Poverty rate (% of population)	2022 EPI Rank
BEN	154	27.1	2.3	51.0	38.5	155
BFA	220	18.4	9.0	68.8	41.4	127
CIV	115	21.1	2.0	47.8	39.5	138
CPV	107	4.9	11.5	32.9	12.3	91
GHA	230	18.9	9.5	42.0	23.4	170
GIN	154	25.8	4.1	62.7	47.7	98
GMB	83	21.2	2.8	36.8	48.6	122
GNB	82	30.9	10.5	55.4	43.7	146
LBR	48	41.1	15.7	47.4	41.9	174
MLI	161	36.2	9.4	55.3	50.9	159
NER	184	38.4	5.6	83.2	40.8	110
NGA	189	24.1	6.2	47.3	40.1	162
SEN	132	16.2	3.2	51.4	46.7	136
SLE	180	59.5	7.8	56.6	56.8	140
TGO	119	18.8	4.3	56.6	55.1	135

Note: GDP and population data refer to 2021; value added shares and natural resource rents to 2020; and poverty rates range from 2016-2021 depending on survey year. EPI = Environmental Performance Index.
Source: Authors' elaboration based on World Bank (2023[2]); UNDP-OPHI (2022[3]); and Wolf et al. (2022[1]).

Figure 5.1. Forest cover as a share of land area in ECOWAS, 1990-2020

Percentage of total land area (%)

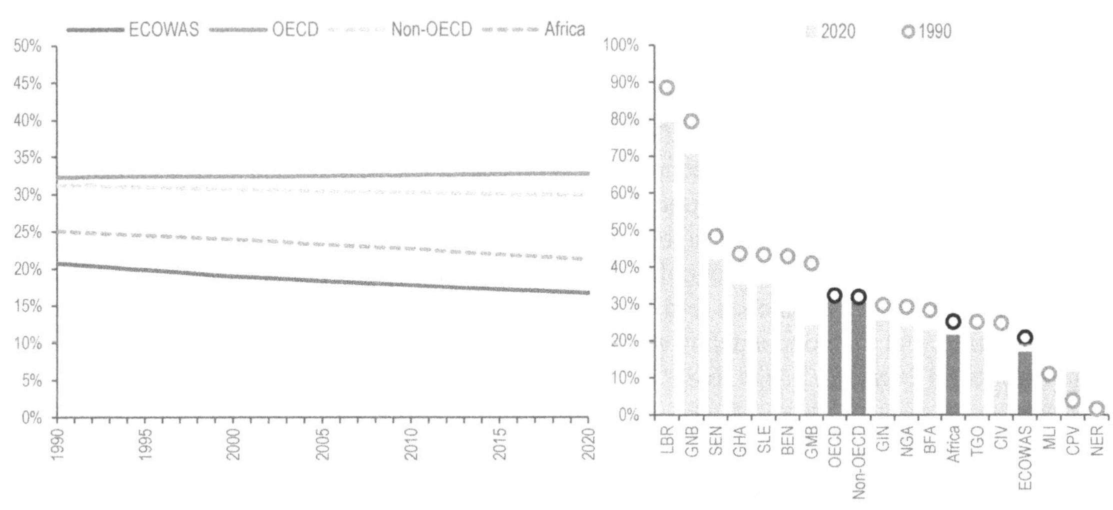

Source: FAO (2022[4]), Agri-environmental indicators – Land use, http://www.fao.org/faostat/, accessed 6.02.23.

West Africa's land, forests, rivers and coasts support employment and livelihoods for most of the region's people and are especially critical for continued progress on reducing poverty. Over 40% of the region's population lives in extreme poverty and over half of the population lives in rural areas (Table 5.1). The number of people living in poverty is particularly high in remote rural areas where peoples' livelihoods rely on small-scale agriculture, fisheries and forest resources. With approximately 400 million people, and an estimated growth rate of 2.75%, the region's population is projected to exceed on billion by 2059. Escalating deforestation, soil degradation, biodiversity loss and over-exploitation of wild-life, fisheries and rangelands undermine the development prospects for present and future generations in many ECOWAS countries.

Figure 5.2. Carbon emissions in West Africa

CO_2 / GDP (kgCO_2 per 2015 US$)

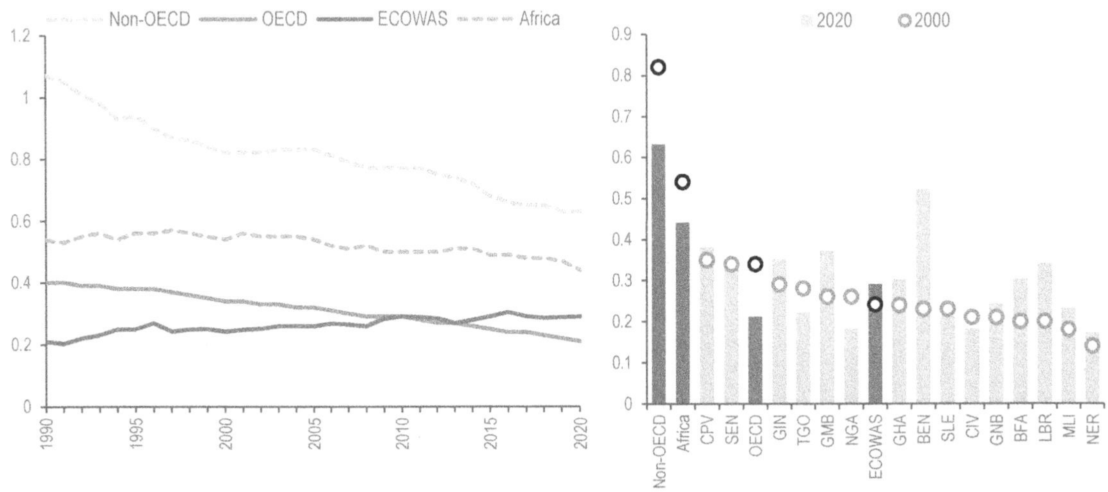

Source: Authors' elaboration based on IEA Greenhouse Gas Emissions from Energy database (2022[5])

West Africa remains highly vulnerable to climate change

The developmental challenges facing ECOWAS countries, exacerbated by poor economic and political governance, make the region highly susceptible to the effects of climate change. Over the last three decades, extreme weather and climate-related disasters have increased in frequency and severity in West Africa. According to the Emergency Events Database, floods and droughts remain the most dominant and devastating disaster events in the region, affecting 70% of the population at least once every two years. The 15 ECOWAS Member States have recorded 22% of all weather-related disasters in Africa in the past four decades. These affected 143 million people, left 2.8 million homeless and inflicted damage in excess of US$ 6.7 billion (UCLouvain, 2023[6]). Climate change is expected to increase the frequency and intensity of extreme hazards such as floods, droughts, storms and wildfires, damaging infrastructure, destroying agricultural crops, disrupting livelihoods and causing loss of lives. Many communities in the region have little ability to adapt, and their dependency on natural resources and exposure to repeated and extreme hazards render them extremely vulnerable.

The Notre Dame-Global Adaptation Index (ND-GAIN) measures the predisposition of countries to be negatively impacted by climate-related hazards across life-supporting sectors, like water, food, health, and infrastructure (i.e. vulnerability), against their economic, social and governance ability to make effective use of investments for adaptation actions thanks to a safe and efficient business environment (i.e. readiness). The index suggests that almost all ECOWAS countries exhibit high levels of vulnerability combined with low levels of readiness, with Niger, Guinea-Bissau, Liberia and Mali among the least resilient (Figure 5.3). With somewhat lower levels of vulnerability and significantly higher readiness, Cabo Verde is the only ECOWAS country considered to be resilient to the effects of climate change.

Figure 5.3. Resilience to climate change in ECOWAS

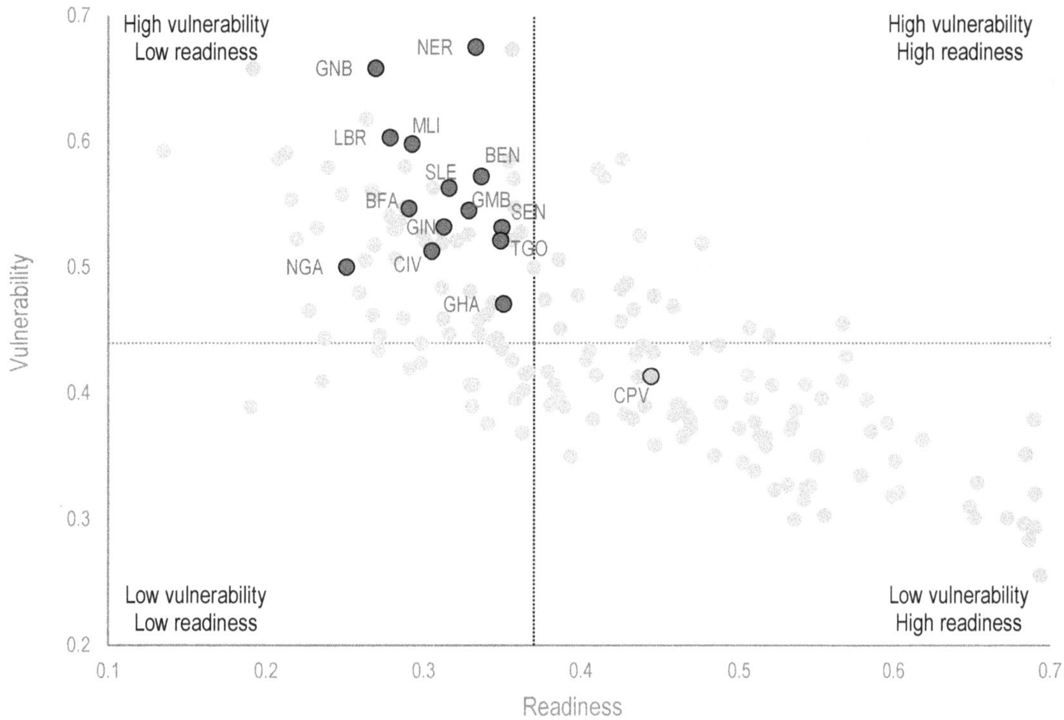

Source: Authors' elaboration based on ND-GAIN Index (2022[7]).

FDI can improve access to clean and affordable energy in the region

Access to energy remains a challenge in West Africa where many countries are dependent on expensive fossil fuels. Despite improvements in electrification over the last two decades, access to electricity in West Africa is at 50%, on average, and at 31% in rural areas (Figure 5.4). Less than 10% of the rural populations of Liberia and Sierra Leone have access to electricity. The region is subject to power shortages of up to 80 hours per month, and electricity costs that are twice the global average, at US$ 0.25 per kilowatt-hour. Russia's invasion of Ukraine has sent food, energy and other commodity prices soaring, increasing the strains on ECOWAS economies already hard hit by the Covid-19 pandemic. Domestic demand in West African countries is often too low to attract investments in large projects that benefit from economies of scale. Instead, these countries rely on small-scale, expensive oil-fired power generation.

Improving access to cleaner and more reliable energy is critical for the provision of health and education services, and plays an important role in poverty reduction and the promotion of economic growth. West Africa's continued progress toward sustainable development will require enormous investment in climate-aligned energy infrastructure. Private investment, and in particular FDI, can play a key role in supporting rural electrification, while also advancing the energy transition of ECOWAS countries. Greenfield FDI is responsible for 30% if new investments in renewable energy, globally, and as multinational enterprises are key players in the deployment of capital- and R&D-intensive clean energy technologies across borders (OECD, 2022[8]).

In West Africa, fossil fuels have attracted the bulk of greenfield FDI flows in the energy sector since 2003. Yet, there has been a substantial rise in renewable energy FDI paralleled by a significant decline in fossil fuels investments in the last decade, and this trend is expected to continue (Figure 5.5). The variation across countries is wide. In Guinea-Bissau, Niger, and Benin, fossil fuels account for over 50% of total greenfield FDI accumulated since 2003, and over 96% of FDI stocks in the energy sector. In Guinea, Senegal, Ghana and Nigeria, fossil fuel FDI is also substantial and accounts for over 80% of FDI in the energy sector. Conversely, in Togo, Mali, the Gambia, Burkina Faso and Sierra Leone, virtually all FDI in the energy sector goes to renewable energy, which accounts for between 8% and 13% of the overall greenfield FDI stock. These countries also have the lowest levels of rural electrification, suggesting that scaling up renewable energy FDI is essential for reducing energy poverty and promoting sustainable development.

Figure 5.4. Electrification remains low in rural parts of West Africa

Percentage of population with access to electricity (%)

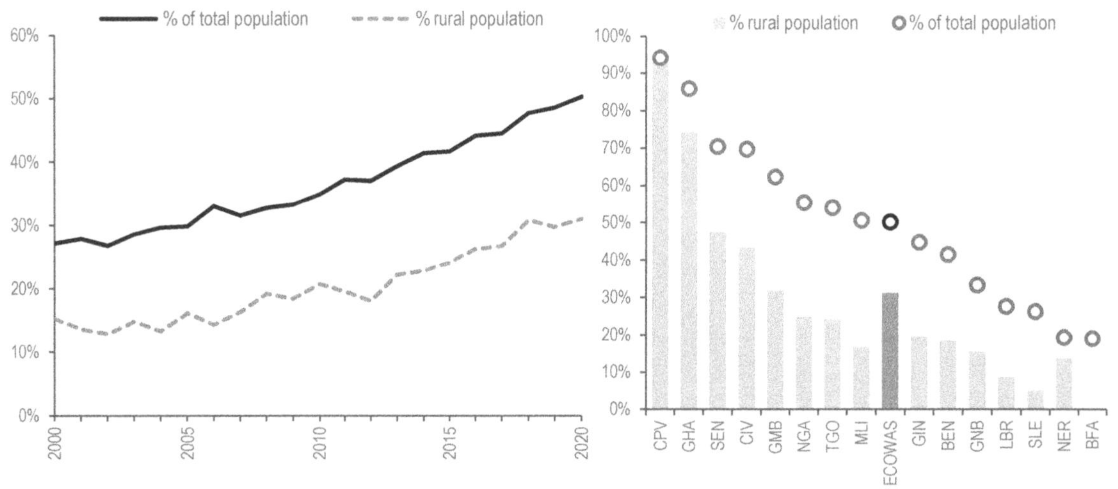

Source: World Bank Global Electrification Database (2023[2])

Figure 5.5. FDI in renewable energy is rising

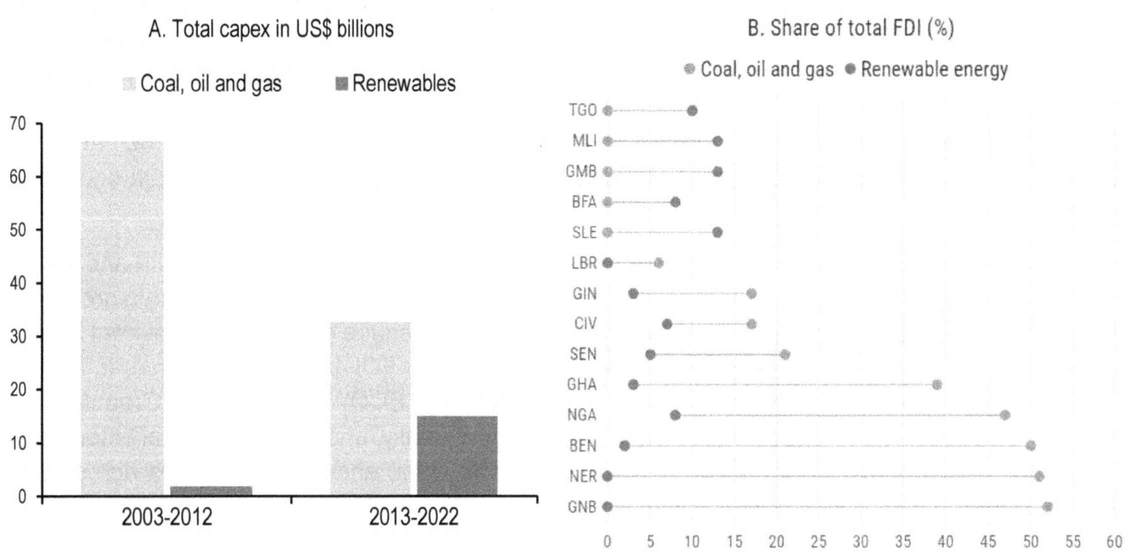

Note: Figure B is calculated using greenfield FDI flows accumulated over 2003-2022.

Source: OECD based on Financial Times (2022[9]) FDI Markets Database.

Policy framework for green growth and climate change

Strong government commitment to combat climate change and to support low-carbon growth, underpinned by a coherent policy framework and clear decarbonisation targets, provides investors with encouraging signals regarding the government's climate ambitions. Setting a clear, long-term transition trajectory that is linked to the national vision or goals for growth and development is critically important to build capacity for investors to understand transition risks, and to attracting foreign investment that contributes to the country's climate agenda.

International commitments to green growth and climate action

ECOWAS recognises the importance of sustainable use and management of the environment in the fight against poverty and energy and food insecurity. ECOWAS Member States have committed themselves to integrated and sustainable development, and climate change adaptation and mitigation. This commitment is reflected by the ECOWAS Treaty establishing the organisation, and active participation in the negotiations and ratification of major Multilateral Environmental Agreements (MEAs). All ECOWAS Member States have ratified the three Rio Conventions: the Convention on Biological Diversity, the United Nations Convention to Combat Desertification (UNCCD), and the United Nations Framework Convention on Climate Change (UNFCCC). There is, however, currently a lack of cohesive regional target-setting across all three Rio Conventions within ECOWAS. These targets are often expressed differently between countries, while the level of detail varies in terms of commitments and implementation plans.

In addition to the Rio Conventions, ECOWAS members have ratified or acceded to most major global MEAs on biodiversity, climate and atmosphere, land and water resources, and chemicals and waste, though some exceptions remain (Table 5.2). ECOWAS members have overwhelmingly ratified most MEAs on biodiversity and migratory species, yet only Liberia has ratified the Lusaka Agreement on Co-operative Enforcement Operations Directed at Illegal Trade in Wild Fauna and Flora, which is the only existing co-operative enforcement instrument assisting the implementation of other biodiversity related agreements at regional level. Four countries in the region have yet to accede to the Bamako Convention on the import of hazardous waste into Africa (Cabo Verde, Ghana, Guinea amd Nigeria), and two countries to the Minamata convention on Mercury (Cabo Verde and Liberia), remaining potentially vulnerable to illegal dumping of spent chemicals, hazardous wastes and banned pesticides. Less than half of ECOWAS members have ratified the UN Watercourses Convention, each ECOWAS country (with the exception of Cabo Verde) shares at least one watercourse with one of its neighbours, suggesting a high degree of interdependence of West African countries with respect to water and a need for collaborative sustainable management of shared water resources.

As of 2019, all ECOWAS Member States signed and ratified the Paris Agreement under the UNFCCC and submitted their Nationally Determined Contributions (NDCs) to the convention, joining the global collaborative effort to mitigate and adapt to climate change. All ECOWAS members have committed to reducing their GHG emissions, albeit to varying degrees, and all countries in the region have submitted updated NDCs, in line with the five-year cycle mandated by the Paris Agreement. These updated NDCs have universally strengthened or added sectoral targets for GHG emissions reductions, as well as strengthening or adding climate policies and actions. In all but one country the updated NDCs offer more information for clarity, transparency and understanding. Only ten revised NDCs strengthened the adaptation component while only five have reduced the total emissions target for 2030.

Table 5.2. Multilateral environmental agreements (MEAs) ratified by ECOWAS Member States

Year of ratification / accession

MEA	BEN	BFA	CPV	CIV	GMB	GHA	GIN	GNB	LBR	MLI	NER	NGA	SEN	SLE	TGO
Biological diversity															
AEWA	2000	2013		2013	2000	2005	2000	2007		2000	2000	2004	2000		2000
Cartagena Protocol	2005	2003	2006	2015	2004	2003	2008	2010	2003	2003	2004	2003	2004	2020	2004
Convention on Biodiversity	1994	1993	1995	1995	1994	1994	1993	1996	2001	1995	1995	1994	1995	1995	1996
CITES	1984	1990	2005	1995	1977	1976	1981	1990	1981	1994	1975	1975	1977	1995	1979
Convention on Migratory Species	1986	1990	2006	2003	2001	1988	1993	1995	2005	1987	1984	1987	1988		1996
Lusaka Agreement									2005						
Nagoya Protocol	2014	2014		2014	2014	2019	2014	2014	2015	2016	2014	2022	2016	2017	2016
Chemicals and waste															
Bamako Convention	2016	2009		1998	2000			2019	2013	1998	1998		1998	2020	1998
Basel Convention	1998	2000	1999	1995	1998	2003	1995	2005	2004	2001	1998	1992	1993	2017	2004
Minamata Convention	2017	2017		2019	2017	2017	2017	2019		2017	2017	2018	2017	2017	2017
Rotterdam Convention	2004	2004	2006	2004	2004	2004	2004	2008	2004	2004	2006	2004	2004	2017	2004
Stockholm Convention	2004	2005	2006	2004	2006	2004	2008	2007	2004	2004	2006	2004	2004	2004	2004
Climate and atmosphere															
Kyoto Protocol	2005	2005	2006	2007	2005	2005	2005	2006	2005	2005	2005	2005	2005	2007	2005
Montreal Protocol	1993	1989	2001	1993	1990	1992	1992	2003	1996	1995	1993	1989	1993	2001	1991
Paris Agreement	2016	2017	2017	2016	2017	2016	2016	2019	2018	2016	2016	2017	2016	2016	2017
UNFCCC	1994	1994	1995	1995	1994	1995	1994	1996	2003	1995	1995	1994	1995	1995	1995
Vienna Convention	1993	1989	2001	1993	1990	1989	1992	2003	1996	1995	1993	1989	1993	2001	1991
Land and water resources															
Ramsar Convention	2000	1990	2005	1996	1996	1988	1993	1990	2003	1987		2000	1977	2000	1995
UNCCD	1996	1996	1996	1997	1996	1997	1997	1996	1998	1996	1996	1997	1996	1997	1996
UN Watercourses Convention	2014	2014		2014		2020		2014			2014	2014			
UN Convention on the Law of the Sea	1998	2005	1994	1994	1994	1994	1994	1994	2008	1994	2013	1994	1994	1995	1994

Source: Authors' elaboration based on https://www.informea.org/en.

Collectively ECOWAS NDCs are not yet aligned with the objectives of the Paris Agreement of limiting the increase in global average temperature to well below 2°C. Only three countries in the region (Cabo Verde, the Gambia and Liberia) have committed to achieving net-zero GHG emissions by 2050, and Nigeria as committed to reach net-zero by 2060 (Table 5.3). Emissions reduction targets are specified in ways that are not directly comparable across countries, due to different time frames and business-as-usual scenarios. Thirteen countries have both an unconditional target, and a significantly more ambitious conditional target, and Mali and Sierra Leone only commit to emissions reductions conditional on international support. The conditions of these targets differ across countries, but frequently include access to international aid in the form of financial resources, technology transfer and capacity building.

Benin, the Gambia and Nigeria are the only countries to have submitted long-term strategy documents in addition to their NDCs. Ambitious long-term low-emission development strategies are vital since current near-term NDCs are only sufficient to limit warming to 2.7-3.7°C. Moreover, long-term strategies provide a pathway to a whole-of-society transformation and a vital link between shorter-term NDCs and the long-term objectives of the Paris Agreement. Given the 30-year time horizon, these strategies offer many other benefits, including guiding countries to avoid costly investments in high-emissions technologies, supporting just and equitable transitions, promoting technological innovation, planning for new sustainable infrastructure in light of future climate risks, and sending early and predictable signals to investors about envisaged long-term societal changes.

Table 5.3. NDC targets of ECOWAS Members

GHG reduction targets relative to Business-As-Usual (BAU) levels

MS	Unconditional target	Conditional target	Net-Zero Target	Sector Targets
BEN	3.6% by 2030	16.1% by 2030	None	AFOLU, energy
BFA	19.6 by 2030	29.4 by 2030	None	AFOLU, energy, transport, waste
CPV	18% by 2030	24% by 2030	2050	Energy, transport, tourism, waste, AFOLU
CIV	30.4% by 2030	98.9% by 2030	None	Energy, agriculture, forestry, waste
GMB	2.6% by 2030	49.7% by 2030	2050	Energy, AFOLU, transport, waste, IPPU
GHA	24.6 MtCO2eq by 2030	39.4 MtCO2eq by 2030	None	Forestry, transport, energy, IPPU, waste
GIN	20% by 2030	49% by 2030	None	Energy, transport, mining, waste, FOLU
GNB	10% by 2030	30% by 2030	None	Energy, waste, AFOLU
LBR	10% by 2030	64% by 203	2050	AFOLU, coastal zones, health, fisheries, transport, industry, energy, waste
MLI	None	39% by 2030	None	energy, AFOLU, waste
NER	12.6% (AFOLU) and 10.6% (Energy) by 2030	22.8% (AFOLU) and 45% (Energy) by 2030	None	Energy, AFOLU
NGA	20% by 2030	47% by 2030	2060	Energy, AFOLU, waste, IPPU
SEN	7% by 2030	29% by 2030	None	Energy, AFOLU, waste, IPPU
SLE	Not specified	25% by 2050	None	Energy, IPPU, waste, transport, AFOLU, blue economy
TGO	20.5% by 2030	50.6% by 2050	None	Energy, AFOLU, IPPU, waste

Note: Details on the conditions of the targets can be found in the source. BAU scenarios and base years vary by country. IPPU = Industrial Processes and Product Use; AFOLU = Agriculture, Forestry and Other Land Use; RAC = Refrigeration and Air Conditioning.
Source: NDCs were retrieved from the official registry (https://www4.unfccc.int/sites/ndcstaging/Pages/Home.aspx).

Policy framework for environmental protection

ECOWAS countries have recognised the mutually reinforcing relationship between human rights and environmental rule of law. The constitutions of nine ECOWAS Members explicitly state the right to a healthy or balanced environment, while another four (the Gambia, Ghana, Nigeria and Sierra Leone) contain clauses to ensure the protection of the environment and natural resources by the State and its citizens. The constitution of Guinea-Bissau refers to the population's right to a "balanced insertion" in its socio-ecological environment in the context of public health but does not explicitly mention environmental protection, while Liberia's constitution omits environmental rights altogether.

West African countries made great strides in formalising EIA into their legal frameworks, with all ECOWAS Member States having promulgated laws in this regard. Four countries in ECOWAS, Cabo Verde, Guinea, Guinea-Bissau and Nigeria, do not have any specific EIA regulations, but have detailed guidelines for the EIA process in the corresponding acts. ECOWAS Members have adopted the same general approach to EIA, which is mandated under an environmental agency (e.g. the Ministry of Environment). EIA processes consist of similar procedures in line with principles set out by the International Association for Impact Assessment (IAIA), involving screening, scoping, impact assessment, approval, and monitoring. The exception is Sierra Leone, where the Environmental Protection Agency Act does not mention scoping. With few exceptions, laws and policies of ECOWAS countries provide for the three critical procedural rights of access to information, public participation, and access to remedies, including grievance redress mechanisms and other project specific complaints processes (Table 5.4). These procedural rights are necessary to ensure that EIAs can effectively identify community concerns about development projects, and therefore critical for environmental governance. They also ensure that the human rights obligations to a clean and safe environment are protected.

Table 5.4. Common elements of EIA systems in ECOWAS

	Year of Act / Regulation	Screening list	Public participation	Access to information	Access to justice	EMP & monitoring	SEA	Transboundary EIA	Certified consultants
BEN	1998 / 2017	■	◘	■	□	■	■	□	■
BFA	2013 / 2015	■	■	■	■	■	■	□	□
CPV	2020	■	■	■	■	■	□	□	■
CIV	1996 / 1996	■	◘	■	◘	◘	■	◘	◘
GMB	1994/ 2014	■	◘	■	■	□	□	◘	□
GHA	1994 / 1999	■	■	■	■	■	◘	◘	□
GIN	2019	■	◘	■	■	■	◘	□	□
GNB	2010/ 2017	■	◘	■	◘	◘	□	■	□
LBR	2003 / 2006	■	■	■	■	◘	□	■	□
MLI	2021 / 2018	■	◘	■	□	■	■	□	□
NER	2018 / 2000	■	◘	■	■	◘	◘	□	□
NGA	1992	■	◘	■	■	◘	◘	◘	◘
SEN	2001/ 2001	■	■	■	□	◘	◘	◘	■
SLE	2022 / 2010	■	◘	■	■	□	□	□	□
TGO	2008 / 2017	■	■	■	■	■	□	◘	◘

Note: ■ = Clear legal requirement in EIA laws and regulations; ◘ = Partial legal requirement (e.g. no regulations or guidelines); □ = No legal requirement. SEA = Strategic Environmental Assessment; EMP = Environmental Management Plan.
Source: Authors based on national EIA legislation and Walmsley and Patel (2020[10]).

EIA processes are most effective where key interested and affected parties are consulted at an early stage of the process, and empowered to contribute to assessing alternatives, identifying community issues and concerns and ensuring that these are addressed in the EIA report. While some level of public consultation is required as part of the EIA process in all ECOWAS countries, the timing and mode of consultation vary significantly. The scope of participation ranges from full engagement of interested and affected parties through various means, including public meetings and focus groups (e.g. in Senegal), to the passive placement of the EIA report for public review and comment (e.g. in Sierra Leone). It is generally considered best practice to consult the public as early in the EIA process as possible, that is, in the scoping phase. Six ECOWAS countries (Burkina Faso, Cabo Verde, Ghana, Liberia, Senegal and Togo) require this. Nine ECOWAS countries require the proponent to undertake public participation during the preparation phase of the EIA. In Benin, Côte d'Ivoire, Guinea-Bissau and Sierra Leone, the authorities will hold public hearings as the sole means of public consultation, while in Guinea there are no regulations or guidelines on specific measures to be followed for public participation and consultation.

Lack of effective post-EIA follow-up and implementation of an Environmental Management Plan (EMP) reduces the value of the EIA process. In almost all ECOWAS countries, the EIA must include measures setting out how the proponent proposes to avoid, reduce, manage or control the adverse impacts of the development on the environment in an EMP. In addition to mandating and offering guidance on EMP formulation, EIA laws should lay out obligations and procedures for monitoring compliance with the EMP. Five ECOWAS countries make provisions for inspections, audits and monitoring by the authorities. In practice this is seldom achieved due to a range of factors including lack of public sector resources. Côte d'Ivoire and Niger place the responsibility for project compliance monitoring and auditing solely on the proponent, who is required to submit regular monitoring and auditing reports to the authorities. This approach requires that the project proponent take ownership of the environmental monitoring process and the management of related risk. Eight countries formally require joint monitoring and auditing, with the proponent doing the day-to day compliance monitoring activities, and the authorities carrying out periodic inspections. This approach is most effective in ensuring compliance with EMPs.

Strategic environmental assessment (SEA) continues to gain momentum, and much of the newer legislation requires SEAs for policies, plans and programmes, notably in seven ECOWAS countries (Benin, Burkina Faso, Côte d'Ivoire, Guinea, Mali, Niger, Senegal). Of these only Benin, Burkina Faso, Côte d'Ivoire and Mali additionally elaborate on the administrative process to be followed and the content of the SEA report in corresponding regulations. In Ghana the legal requirement for SEA is weak, with plans and programmes included in the "undertakings" for which environmental assessments are required. Nevertheless, non-statutory guidelines for the "Ghana SEA Approach" have been developed and over 20 SEAs have been conducted in the last decade, on a range of proposed policies and plans. In Nigeria there a SEA guideline document published by the Federal Ministry of Environment, and SEA is provided for in the draft EIA bill. In Gambia there is only a fleeting mention to SEAs in the EIA Regulations, while no mention of SEAs is made in the environmental laws of the remaining ECOWAS countries.

The application of EIA principles to the assessment of transboundary impacts of investment remains limited in ECOWAS, and only Guinea-Bissau and Liberia provide a legal framework for the control and restriction of any contaminants that may have a cross-border effect or regional. In Senegal and Togo, environmental authorities are required to initiate a consultative process with the relevant authorities of countries that may be significantly adversely affected by a proposed activity. In Côte d'Ivoire, Gambia, Ghana and Nigeria, the EIA report must include an indication of whether the environment of any other State is likely to be affected by the proposed project and what mitigation measures are to be undertaken, but there is no reference to consultation with the concerned countries. All other ECOWAS countries do not require transboundary EIA in their environmental laws, but may be signatories to trans-boundary agreements which require sharing of information, as well as some trans-frontier conservation initiatives.

Ensuring a high level of professional quality and conduct of EIA practitioners is central to the effectiveness of the EIA process, and for this reason, it is good practice to introduce a certification scheme for EIA practitioners and consultants. At present, only Benin, Cabo Verde, and Senegal have a statutory requirement for certification of environmental assessment practitioners. Côte d'Ivoire, Nigeria and Togo have put in place registration systems for EIA practitioners based on professional criteria, which also afford some degree of quality control. The Gambia and Mali require EIA consultants and their qualifications to be sent to the authorities for approval before commencing the EIA, affording a lower level of quality control that hinges on the accuracy of the information provided by the consultants. The lowest level of quality assurance is provided in Burkina Faso, Guinea, Liberia and Niger, where the environmental agency has a list of approved consultants. In Ghana, Guinea-Bissau and Sierra Leone there is no certification or registration system for EIA practitioners. There is, therefore, little control over the professionalism and conduct of EIA consultants in the region.

Policy approaches to promote green investment

Uncertainty and unpredictability are among the greatest barriers to green investment. Too often the reason governments fail to attract green investment is due to the lack of an enabling environment for investment. Green investors are no different than any other in requiring a stable, predictable, and transparent investment environment in which to identify bankable projects. Thus, efforts to mobilise green investment will fail to meet their intended target unless governments ensure a regulatory climate that provides investors with fair treatment and confidence in the rule of law. The widely accepted features of this enabling environment are detailed in the OECD Policy Framework for Investment (PFI).

At the same time, openness, stability, and fair treatment are not enough to channel private investment towards green growth and decarbonisation objectives. In other words, policies conducive to FDI will not automatically result in a substantial increase in green or climate-aligned FDI. Policymakers will also need to improve specific enabling conditions for green investment by developing policies and regulations that systematically internalise the cost of environmental externalities like carbon emissions. Targeted financial, technical and information support can also help address market failures that reduce the competitiveness of climate-aligned investments.

Stimulating investment in green technologies

Private investors do not internalise the positive spillovers of low-carbon investments and are likely to under-invest in related technologies and skills compared to socially optimal levels. Targeted financial and technical support by the government is therefore warranted but must be transparent, time-limited and subject to regular review. Studies have shown that the variations in the cost-effectiveness of these technology support policies depend on the country context rather than on the specific tool used. In general, government support should decrease over time as the technology matures (OECD, 2022[11]). As noted previously, FDI in renewable energy is picking up in some West African countries, but still considerably lags behind FDI in fossil fuels overall. Targeted measures to accelerate investments in the renewable energy sector can be an effective way to decarbonise the region and promote green growth.

Many ECOWAS Member States have put in place incentives for renewable energy products and technologies. The most widely used forms of financial support include subsidies and grants for electrification programmes, tax exemptions on renewable energy equipment and generation, and tariff-based schemes like public auctions, feed-in-tariffs and net-metering schemes (Table 5.5). Only Nigeria is in the process of developing a voluntary carbon offset market.

Table 5.5. Financial support for renewable energy

	Subsidies	Tax incentives	Tariff-based schemes	Carbon markets
BEN	Green bond	Import tax, VAT	Auctions, Net-metering	None
BFA	RE Fund	CIT, Import tax, VAT	Auctions	None
CPV	Loan subsidy	CIT, Import tax,	Auctions	None
CIV	SEP	Import tax, VAT	Auctions	None
GMB	SEP	CIT, Import tax, VAT	Feed-in tariff, Net-metering	None
GHA	RE Fund, Loan subsidy, SEP	CIT, Import tax, VAT	Net-metering, Feed-in tariff (repealed 2020)	None
GIN		None	None	None
GNB	SEP	CIT, Import tax, VAT	None	None
LBR	RE Fund	Import tax, VAT	Auctions	None
MLI		Import tax, VAT	Auctions	None
NER	SEP	Import tax, VAT	Auctions	None
NGA	RE Fund, Loan subsidy, SEP	None	Feed-in tariff	Under development
SEN	RE fund, SEP	VAT	Net-metering	None
SLE	SEP	Import tax	Auctions	None
TGO	SEP	CIT, Import tax	Auctions, Net-metering	None

Note: CIT = Corporate Income Tax; REP = Solar Electrification Programme; RE = Renewable Energy; VAT = Value Added Tax.
Source: OECD FDI Qualities Mapping

With few exceptions, all ECOWAS countries offer some form of subsidy for renewable energy investments, in the form of funds or grants, electrification programmes, or subsidised loans. Various types of funds that offer capital and production-based subsidies to renewable energy developers are found in Burkina Faso (Green Energy Fund), Ghana (REFUND), Liberia (REFUND) and Senegal (RE & EE Fund). Eight ECOWAS countries seek to increase renewable energy capacity through solar electrification programmes (SEPs). Several of these programmes in Niger (PRODERE, ROGEP, Haske Electrification Programme), Guinea-Bissau (GEF Project), Ghana (RESPRO, Solar Rooftop Programme), and Nigeria (Energizing Economies Initiative) involve the direct the installation of mini-power plants and photovoltaic solar kits in rural and peri-urban areas. Three ECOWAS Member States have put in place measures to increase access to credit to finance renewable energy investments: Ghana's SUNREF initiative offers long-term, low interest rate financing to local commercial banks for on-lending to renewable energy and energy efficiency projects; Nigeria's Green SME Financing initiative provides exclusive credit lines credit lines to finance eligible green SME; and Cabo Verde provides interest rate support of 50% for micro production of renewable energies. Benin is the first country in the region to have launched an SDG bond to help finance, among others, renewable energy projects.

The most widely used tax incentives to promote renewable energy include import tax and VAT exemptions on related machinery and equipment, provided by the majority of ECOWAS countries. Togo and Cabo Verde also offer credits and deductions from corporate income tax (CIT) for qualifying investments in the renewable energy sector, which have the advantage of reducing initial capital costs. Burkina Faso, the Gambia and Ghana offer corporate income tax (CIT) holidays ranging 4-15 years, which are potentially very costly in terms of forgone revenues (see Chapter 4). The Gambia and Ghana simultaneously offer similar CIT tax reductions for investments in fossil fuels, while another six ECOWAS Member States offer CIT holidays only to fossil fuels. Moreover, in Mali and Nigeria these exemptions are permanent. These types of incentives erode the tax base and reduce the ultimate effectiveness of efforts to promote clean energy investment (Figure 5.6). These countries would benefit from categorising green and non-green activities according to emerging taxonomies and phasing out or scaling down financial and fiscal incentives granted to non-green activities, while implementing more targeted measures to ensure energy access and affordability.

Tariff-based schemes have become an integral part of policy instruments to promote renewable energy investment in West Africa, and are provided by all ECOWAS Members with the exception of Guinea and Guinea-Bissau. These instruments reduce the risk of private investments by guaranteeing a predetermined price (or tariff) for the electricity generated for a predefined period of time. Feed-in tariff regimes have been put in place by the Gambia, Ghana and Nigeria (though later repealed in Ghana) and are typically combined with guaranteed access to the grid for renewable generators. A key drawback of these regimes is that setting the right tariff is a complex exercise with the rapidly decreasing cost of the technologies, particularly in young markets where government capacity in the design of feed-in tariffs may be low and there may be asymmetry of information between regulators and companies. Indeed, there has been evidence of limited effectiveness of Malawi's feed-in tariff regime (OECD, forthcoming[12]). Public auctions have the advantage of overcoming such informational asymmetries and promoting cost efficiency by allowing for a market-based determination of tariffs. This has led most ECOWAS countries to opt for auctioning renewable capacity to determine the price of the feed-in tariff. While auctions are well-suited for established projects, they transfer higher risk to investors, and a number of Southern African countries (Malawi, Namibia, South Africa, Zambia) opt for a hybrid approach combining feed-in tariffs and auctions (OECD, 2023[13]).

Net metering is a billing mechanism that credits solar energy system owners for the electricity they add to the grid. Customers also benefit from reduced electricity bills through self-consumption of the electricity they produce. As such, net metering schemes can be a vital policy option to encourage community-based small scale renewable energy producers, while also encouraging energy efficiency. Growing populations and increasing shares of SMEs in West Africa have amplified the demand for small-scale decentralised renewable energy projects, yet only four West African countries (Benin, Gambia, Senegal and Togo) have put in place net-metering frameworks. In order to be effective, these schemes could be accompanied by subsidies to set up solar installations. For instance, in Ghana, the Solar Rooftop Programme subsidises investments in rooftop solar panels to encourage solar self-consumption, while any excess production of renewable energy can be added to the grid to benefit from the net-metering compensation scheme.

Figure 5.6. Tax incentives continue to favour fossil fuels

Maximum number of years of CIT exemption

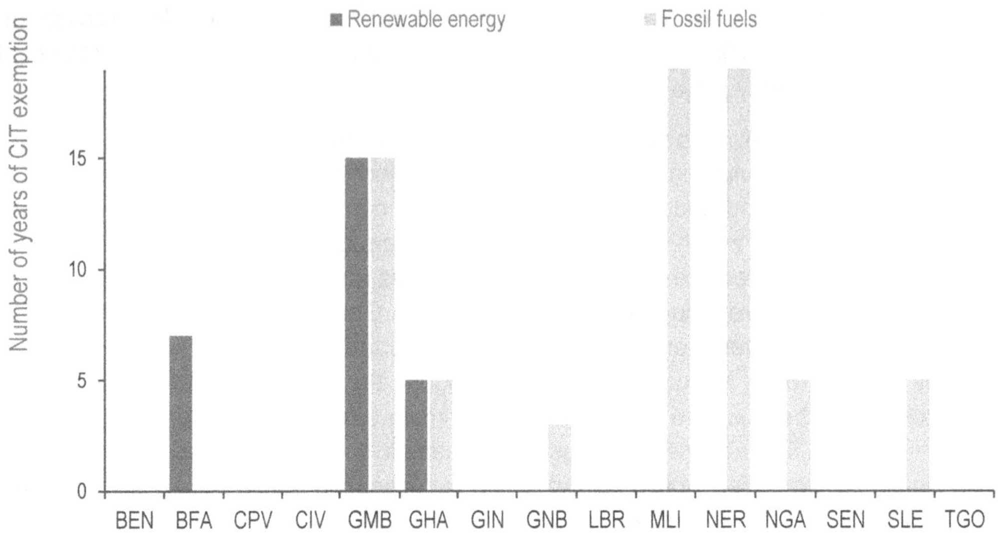

Note: In Mali and Niger, CIT exemptions for fossil fuels are permanent.
Source: OECD elaboration

Building green capabilities and addressing informational barriers to green investment

Technical support is a useful tool for reducing the environmental footprint of investments, building capabilities related to green technologies, and promoting green innovation and spillovers. The majority of ECOWAS countries offer technical support to develop renewable energy capabilities, in particular of workers, often delivered in partnership with development cooperation agencies (Table 5.6). For instance, the Solar Thermal Training & Demonstration Initiative (SOLTRAIN) is a capacity building programme implemented in Burkina Faso, Ghana, Nigeria, and Senegal, with financial and technical support from the Austrian Development Agency. Similarly, the Green People's Energy for Africa initiative aims to improve the conditions for decentralised energy supply in rural areas in Benin, Côte d'Ivoire, Ghana and Senegal, and is implemented by the Deutsche Gesellschaft fur Internationale (GIZ). Cabo Verde and Côte d'Ivoire also have dedicated renewable energy training centres, while Nigeria offers clean energy qualification courses. Programmes in Gambia (REPGam) and Ghana (Green Programme) seek to enhance the skills potential and employability of youth by offering training on photovoltaic system installation, maintenance and franchising, while Togo's Wenyonu Programme seeks to empower women to become solar entrepreneurs. These kinds of initiatives essential to build capabilities necessary to attract renewable energy investments, and promote spillovers to domestic businesses and entrepreneurs.

Technical support can also be directed towards starting up green businesses, improving the energy and environmental performance of existing businesses, or encouraging green innovation. Five ECOWAS countries (Cabo Verde, Côte d'Ivoire, Ghana, Nigeria, and Togo) have put in place incubators and accelerators tailored to support green start-ups and entrepreneurs. Gambia and Liberia offer business development services that target SMEs to help improve their energy performance or to facilitate technology adoption. While still not present in the region, green special economic zones, industrial parks and technology parks can also be tailored to facilitate green FDI and create green innovation hubs that attract talent and investors. For example, South Africa's Atlantis Greentech Special Economic Zone (SEZ) makes use of a range of investment attraction tools, including streamlined investment facilitation, preferential land use, infrastructure provision, easy access to major transport hubs, and SEZ-specific customs and fiscal regimes to attract investors in green technologies. Moreover, South Africa is striving to develop the first zero solid-waste eco-industrial park in Africa, known as the Limpopo Eco-Industrial Park by improving resource use and fostering industrial synergies in existing industrial parks (OECD, 2023[13]).

Table 5.6. Technical and information support for green investments

MS	Technical support		Information support		
	Training & skills development	*Business & supplier development*	*Green promotion & facilitation*	*Public awareness campaigns*	*Disclosure, certification & labelling*
BEN	RECASEB, Green People's Energy	RECASEB		RECASEB	
BFA	SOLTRAIN, Green Economy Learning Assessment				
CPV	CERMI Training Course, CdC 3C	CERMI Spin-off incubator, CdC 3C	Energy Information Management System		
CIV	Pollution Monitoring & Control, RE Training Centre, Green People's Energy	Incubation Express, uPOPCI	Environmental Information system	PNCC, PNGD, PNGEC, PNGRN, PNGPC	
GMB	REPGam, Greening Productive Sectors	Business Development Services for MSMEs, Empretec Gambia	GIEPA solar energy investment resources		
GHA	Green Programme: Youth Employment, SOLTRAIN, Green People's Energy	Green Programme: Incubation Acceleration, Mentoring	Green Programme Investment Forums	Green Climate Fund for Civil Society	Sustainable Banking Principles
GIN					
GNB	Green Seed Program			GEF Project	
LBR		SME Green Competitiveness	Renewables Liberia		
MLI					
NER	Mainstreaming Climate Change Adaptation	PACRC			
NGA	NAPTIN, Clean Energy Qualification, SOLTRAIN	NCIC Incubation Programme	Green Energy Investment Platform	NCIC Public Events	
SEN	SOLTRAIN, Green People's Energy				
SLE	Renewable Energy Empowerment project		Renewables Sierra Leone, SLIEPA investor guides	Environmental awareness campaign, Power for All	
TGO	Wenyonu Programme, Solar Entrepreneurship Programme	Energy Generation Incubator			

Source: OECD FDI Qualities Mapping

In addition to technical support, information and facilitation services can help reduce informational barriers and asymmetries that lead to sub-optimal investment and consumption choices, and generally result in under-investment in green technologies. For instance, lack of awareness on the energy performance of household appliances leads to an inability of consumers to interpret the impact of energy prices on the operational costs of one product relative to another, meaning that price signals do not influence purchasing behaviour as expected. Measures to raise public awareness and understanding of energy and environmental performance, including information campaigns, product labelling schemes, certification and disclosure requirements can help alleviate these information barriers. Investment promotion and facilitation tools can also help potential investors identify green investment opportunities and overcome related administrative barriers.

Many West African countries have developed effective tools to facilitate access to environmental information and opportunities related to green investments. The most common information tools used to promote green investments in West Africa, include public awareness campaigns and information platforms. In Côte d'Ivoire, for example, various programmes seek to raise awareness among the general public on issues related climate change, waste management, natural resource management and preservation, and dangers associated with chemical products. Nigeria's Climate Innovation Centre hosts public events for awareness raising, especially in opportunities available for green business, entrepreneurship and innovation, while Ghana's Green Climate Fund for Civil Society sponsors public awareness campaigns related to climate action. Campaigns in Benin and Guinea-Bissau focus the importance of energy efficiency and renewable energy to increase energy access and security. In terms of investment information tools, five countries in the region (Cabo Verde, Gambia, Liberia, Nigeria, and Sierra Leone) have put in place platforms that offer detailed information, data and contacts, relating to investment opportunities in the renewable energy sector. Sierra Leone's investment promotion agency also offers investor guides with detailed information on green investment opportunities, while Ghana holds biannual investment forums to bring together potential investors interested in Ghana's green sectors, under its Green Programme.

Voluntary disclosure and reporting of environmental impacts remains limited in West Africa. Nevertheless, in November 2019, the Bank of Ghana launched the Ghana Sustainable Banking Principles to provide the guiding principles to underpin effective Environmental and Social Risk Management policy frameworks for banks, including reporting requirements for five sectors that are critically sensitive to the environmental and social standards. As of 2020, 24 commercial banks in Ghana agreed to measure and report their progress in implementing the principles. Other countries in the region should consider developing frameworks for voluntary disclosure of environmental impacts in critical sectors.

References

FAO (2022), *Agri-environmental indicators - Land use*, http://www.fao.org//faostat/. [4]

Financial Times (2022), *FDI Markets*, https://www.fdimarkets.com/. [9]

IEA (2022), *Greenhouse Gas Emissions from Energy*, https://www.iea.org/data-and-statistics/data-product/greenhouse-gas-emissions-from-energy. [5]

OECD (2023), *Sustainable Investment Policy Perspectives in SADC*, OECD Publishing, Paris. [13]

OECD (2022), *FDI Qualities Indicators 2022*, https://www.oecd.org/investment/fdi-qualities-indicators.htm. [8]

OECD (2022), *FDI Qualities Policy Toolkit*, OECD Publishing, Paris, https://doi.org/10.1787/7ba74100-en. [11]

OECD (forthcoming), *Africa's Development Dynamics 2023*. [12]

UCLouvain (2023), *Natural Disasters Database*, https://public.emdat.be/. [6]

UNDP-OPHI (2022), *Global Multidimensional Poverty Index 2022: Unpacking deprivation bundles to reduce multidimensional poverty*, https://hdr.undp.org/content/2022-global-multidimensional-poverty-index-mpi#/indicies/MPI. [3]

University of Notre Dame (2022), "ND-GAIN Index", https://gain.nd.edu/our-work/country-index/matrix/. [7]

Walmsley, B. and S. Husselman (2020), *Handbook on environmental assessment legislation in selected countries in Sub-Saharan Africa*, Development Bank of Southern Africa (DBSA) and Southern African Institute for Environmental Assessment, https://irp-cdn.multiscreensite.com/2eb50196/files/uploaded/SADC%20Handbook.pdf. [10]

Wolf, M. et al. (2022), *2022 Environmental Performance Index.*, Yale Center for Environmental Law & Policy, http://epi.yale.edu. [1]

World Bank (2023), *World Development Indicators*, https://databank.worldbank.org/. [2]

6 Promoting and enabling responsible business conduct

This chapter first explains the relevance of responsible business conduct (RBC) in the ECOWAS region and the key elements of RBC. It then gives an overview and analysis of policies and initiatives relevant for RBC in ECOWAS at regional and national levels, as well as access to remedy and stakeholder awareness of RBC.

In ECOWAS, policy makers, businesses and civil society have made important steps to foster responsible business conduct (RBC) at both national and regional levels as well as in the extractive and agriculture sectors. Moreover, the ECOWAS institutions have already frameworks and policies in place which build a basis for further uptake and promotion of RBC. However, countries and enterprises have moved forward at different speeds on the RBC agenda. Many related initiatives are still at early stages and gaps remain to implement concrete action and to build capacity on international standards on RBC and risk-based due diligence. This chapter first explains the relevance of RBC in the ECOWAS region and the key elements of RBC. It then gives an overview and analysis of policies and initiatives relevant for RBC in ECOWAS at regional and national levels, as well as access to remedy and stakeholder awareness of RBC.

Promoting RBC to drive trade, investment and sustainable development

In the past decade, different terms such as Corporate Social Responsibility (CSR) and Environmental, Social, and Governance (ESG) have been used to reflect the expectation that businesses should consider non-financial impacts as part of their core business considerations and not as an add-on. RBC is more specific in that it sets out an expectation that all businesses – regardless of their legal status, size, ownership structure or sector – avoid and address negative consequences of their operations, while contributing to sustainable development where they operate. This means considering impacts on people, planet and society such as corruption, environmental, labour or human rights risks within business activities throughout the entire supply chain. Enabling RBC is a key component to attract quality investment, to foster trade and to ensure that business activities contribute to broader value creation and sustainable development.

Relevance of RBC for ECOWAS and its Member States

The importance of enabling and implementing RBC has been recognised internationally from a business, trade and investment perspective. From the business side, enterprises have confirmed that implementing RBC practices and considering risks beyond financial materiality can benefit their own business. Among others, the implementation of due diligence and higher sustainability requirements has proven to make supply chains more resilient to external shocks and crises. For instance, in response to an OECD firm-level survey on RBC in Latin America, 75% of firms indicated that having responsible practices in place such as due diligence has helped them navigate the COVID-19 crisis, notably by mitigating risks (OECD, 2021[1]). A global study by the World Benchmarking Alliance found similar results (WBA, 2021[2]).

In ECOWAS, the implementation of RBC is especially key to the region's economic development given the strategic importance of the mining and agri-food industries for the sustainable development and creation of quality jobs in the region. The food economy, for instance, represents 35% of West Africa's GDP, accounts for 66% of the region's total employment and 10% of total exports. While ECOWAS is home to important natural resources and an abundant labour supply, the integration in global value chains and added value of exported goods remains low compared to other world regions due to persisting barriers and vulnerabilities across supply chains such as low productivity, environmental shocks, and unofficial fees (AUC/OECD, 2022[3]). In the face of these constraints, RBC is an important opportunity to increase ECOWAS' integration in sustainable value chains.

Enabling and implementing RBC can help to gain and maintain export market access, especially in sectors which are subject to environmental, labour and human rights risks such as the minerals, agricultural and garment sectors. This importance is further reinforced by increasing global and regional expectations related to RBC. In the ECOWAS region these expectations are driven notably by regulatory developments in key exports markets such as the EU. These developments will likely impact businesses in ECOWAS, since the EU is West Africa's biggest export market, accounting for 20% of exports in 2020 (EC, 2022[4]; ECOWAS, n.d.[5]). Moreover, the ongoing implementation process of the African Continental Free Trade

Area (AfCFTA) represents a key opportunity to further mainstream RBC in trade relations given the potential socio-economic impacts of a single continental market (UNECA/ FES, 2022[6]).

From an investment perspective, there is evidence that RBC policies including labour standards, tenure rights over natural resources, human rights, anti-corruption and integrity have high potential to attract quality investment. An OECD survey on FDI decisions found that strong and effective laws governing RBC represented the policy area which had the strongest positive effect encouraging investment in foreign agri-food markets (Punthakey, 2020[7]). Regional analysis of panel data across ECOWAS countries has further confirmed that RBC practices, such as improving the efficacy of anti-corruption measures can be instrumental in attracting FDI and its beneficial effects on economic growth (Asante et al., 2022[8]).

The elements of RBC

Globally, there has been a steady rise in expectations on RBC which is reflected by investors and consumers demanding companies to report and act on RBC, and by a rise in benchmarking and lawsuits against companies regarding human rights and environmental impacts. Provisions on RBC are included increasingly in international trade and investment agreements as well as national and regional development strategies, laws, and regulations.

International instruments on RBC

Global expectations on RBC are set out and aligned in three main international instruments – the OECD Guidelines for Multinational Enterprises on Responsible Business Conduct (MNE Guidelines), the UN Guiding Principles on Business and Human Rights (UN Guiding Principles), and the ILO Tripartite Declaration of Principles concerning Multinational Enterprises and Social Policy (Box 6.1).

The MNE Guidelines are the most comprehensive international standard on RBC, providing a set of recommendations to businesses across sectors on responsible conduct in all areas of business ethics, such as governance and disclosure aspects, human rights and labour rights, the environment and climate change, bribery, corruption, consumers' interest or taxation. The MNE Guidelines are part of the OECD Declaration on International Investment and Multinational Enterprises, which, to date, has 51 adherents. All these governments have set up a National Contact Points for Responsible Business Conduct (NCP). The NCPs are agencies established by governments with a twofold mandate: promoting the MNE Guidelines and related due diligence guidance, and handling cases (referred to as "specific instances") as a non-judicial grievance mechanism.

Box 6.1. Overview of main international instruments on RBC

International convergence on RBC principles and standards

The three main instruments that have become key reference points for responsible business, are the OECD Guidelines for Multinational Enterprises on Responsible Business Conduct, the UN Guiding Principles on Business and Human Rights (UNGPs), and the ILO Tripartite Declaration of Principles concerning Multinational Enterprises and Social Policy. They are aligned with and complement each other and set global expectations with regard to responsible conduct. Some of the key areas on which these instruments converge include:

- *Framework for all companies.* International corporate responsibility standards set the expectation that all companies – regardless of their size, sector, operational context, ownership and structure – avoid and address the adverse impacts and contribute to the sustainable development of the countries in which they operate.
- *Common understanding of impact.* The instruments set out that the impact of business activities goes beyond the impact on the company itself and refers to the impact business activities may have on human rights – including labour rights – the environment and society, both positive and negative. The instruments establish a

common understanding that enterprises can cause, contribute to, or be directly linked to adverse impacts, and they provide a framework for how enterprises should avoid and address them.

- *Conducting due diligence.* Businesses should undertake due diligence to identify, prevent and mitigate their actual and potential negative impacts and account for how those impacts are addressed. This process involves meaningful consultation with potentially affected groups and other relevant stakeholders.
- *Responsibility throughout the supply chain.* Responsible business covers not only impacts that a company may cause or contribute to through its own activities but also those impacts directly linked to an enterprise's operations, products or services through its business relationships. This includes business partners, entities in the value chain such as subsidiaries, suppliers, franchisees, joint ventures, investors, clients, contractors, customers, consultants, financial, legal and other advisers, and any other non-state or state entities.
- *Access to remedy.* As part of their duty to protect against business-related adverse impacts, states are expected to take appropriate steps to ensure, through judicial, administrative, legislative or other appropriate means, that when such abuses occur within their territory and/or jurisdiction those affected have access to effective remedy. In addition, where companies identify that they have caused or contributed to adverse impacts, they are expected to address them through providing remedy, and they should provide for or co-operate in this remediation through legitimate processes.

Source: OECD (2023[9]); OECD (2018[10]); OECD (2015[11]); EC (2023[12]); UN-OECD-EU-ILO-SDJW (2019[13]).

Risk-based due diligence

Conducting risk-based due diligence stands at the heart of RBC and means identifying, preventing and mitigating actual and potential adverse impacts, and accounting for how these impacts are addressed. Unlike many traditional corporate risk management and compliance systems that focus on the company's primary risks, such as financial, market, operational or reputation risks, due diligence considers not only the risks to the company, but also risks that companies can cause, contribute to or to which they are linked along the whole supply chain (OECD, 2018[10]).

The OECD Due Diligence Guidance for RBC establishes a six-step process to conduct due diligence that can be translated and used by any enterprise, irrespective of its size, location or sector of its operations (Figure 6.1). This process consists of (1) embedding RBC into the enterprise's policies and management systems, (2) identifying and assessing adverse impacts in operations, supply chains and business relationships, (3) ceasing, preventing or mitigating adverse impacts, (4) tracking implementation and results, (5) communicating how impacts are addressed, and (6) providing for or co-operating in remediation when appropriate. Beyond this cross-sectoral Due Diligence Guidance, the OECD has also developed guidance to provide tailored recommendations in specific sectors, including agriculture, minerals, extractives, garments and footwear, and finance.

Governments around the world are increasingly translating a risk-based due diligence approach into law to enable RBC. Currently 75% of OECD countries have already introduced or are in the process of introducing some sort of regulation embedding requirements of risk-based due diligence including disclosure laws, conduct requirements, and product and trade bans. Several governments such as France, Germany, Switzerland and Norway have been among the first ones to introduce comprehensive legislation, which make it mandatory for companies to carry out effective due diligence processes. At the regional level, the EU adopted a legislative proposal on mandatory due diligence in 2022: the Corporate Sustainability Due Diligence Directive establishes a due diligence duty including both EU and non-EU companies (OECD, n.d.[14]; EC, 2022[4]).

Figure 6.1. The risk-based due diligence process and supporting measures

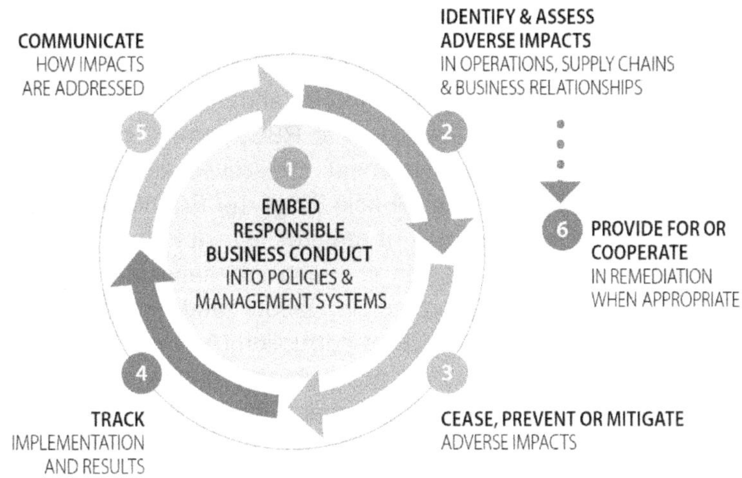

Source: OECD (2018[10]).

Promoting RBC in ECOWAS and its Member States

Implementing responsible business practices requires an enabling policy environment at both national and regional level. Policy makers should establish conditions that effectively drive, support and promote responsible business practices. This means putting in place, maintaining *and* effectively enforcing a legal framework in all relevant areas where business intersects with people, planet and society as laid out in the OECD Recommendation on the Role of Government in Promoting Responsible Business Conduct (OECD, 2023[15]).

Policies and initiatives relevant for RBC at the ECOWAS regional level

Overarching policies at ECOWAS level

ECOWAS members have jointly committed to promoting international standards of RBC in relation to international investment in their countries and have established legal frameworks to guide and harmonise policies among Members States with respect to RBC, notably in the ECOWAS Investment Policy (ECOWIP) and the ECOWAS Investment Code (ECOWIC).

The ECOWAS Investment Policy (ECOWIP, 2017) establishes harmonised regional investment-climate policies for the Member States to maximise the economic and social benefits of regional integration in West Africa in line with global best practices. The ECOWIP includes a Chapter 12 dedicated to RBC and the protection of the environment, which is based on the OECD Policy Framework for Investment (ECOWAS, 2018[16]). It refers to international best practices and RBC standards covering all types of businesses "regardless of their legal nature, size, ownership structure, or sector of the economy in which they operate". It acknowledges the shared responsibility of states and enterprises to promote RBC. The policy principles and strategies in Chapter 12 of the ECOWIP highlight the importance of promoting RBC for sustainable development aligned with the OECD standards for RBC along three objectives: first, "promote sustainable and inclusive economic and social development"; second, "avoid and address any materially adverse impacts (e.g. environmental degradation) caused by business activities"; third, "prevent or mitigate negative effects directly linked to the operations, products, or services of business entities". Among other recommendations and in line with the OECD Policy Framework for Investment, Chapter 12 highlights several ways how governments can enable RBC including regulation, facilitation, co-operation, promotion and exemplification (ECOWAS, 2018[16]).

The ECOWIP represents the foundation of the ECOWIC, which provides the legal framework for the implementation of the investment policy. The ECOWIC lays out rules and principles that govern the admission of international investments within the community and provides guidelines for their exploitation. Various articles of the ECOWIC refer to or are linked to RBC, notably in Chapter 6 "Environment and Sustainable Development", in Chapter 8 "Development, Objectives and Social Responsibility", and in Chapter 9 "Corruption and Unethical Practices". Article 34 of the ECOWIC refers directly to Corporate Governance and Responsible Business Conduct. It requires investors in ECOWAS territory to promote and engage in responsible business practices in line with internationally recognised standards. This includes environmental and human rights protection, labour and employment rights including the elimination of child labour (Article 30) and combatting corruption (Article 38). Article 27 explicitly requires investors doing business in ECOWAS to carry out and publish pre-investment environmental and social impact assessments. Member States are further meant to adopt RBC policies and international environmental standards (ECOWAS, 2018[17]). Despite these clear requirements relating to RBC, it remains an open question whether the ECOWIC provisions are implemented effectively at national level in the Members States (AfDB, 2020[18]).

Thematic policies and initiatives at ECOWAS level

Beyond the ECOWIC and ECOWIP, the Community has put forward a range of policies relating to the role of government in promoting RBC. These policies address the key areas of RBC, notably human and labour rights, children's rights, climate and environment, as well as anti-corruption in line with key international standards and commitments. An overview of the ECOWAS frameworks relevant to RBC is listed in Table 6.1.

Table 6.1. ECOWAS policy frameworks related to RBC

ECOWAS framework	Launch date	Content
ECOWAS Treaty	1975; revised in 1993	Fundamental framework for member countries to drive collaboration, maintain regional peace, protect human rights, and promote economic growth.
ECOWAS Vision 2050	2022	ECOWAS policy directions until 2050
ECOWAS Investment Policy	2018	Policy to promote regional investment and development. Chapter 12 "Responsible Business Conduct and Protection of the Environment"
ECOWAS Common Investment Code	2018	Framework to implement the ECOWAS Investment Policy. Chapter 6 "Environment and Sustainable Development", in Chapter 8 "Development, Objectives and Social Responsibility", and in Chapter 9 "Corruption and Unethical Practices". Article 34 "Corporate Governance and Responsible Business Conduct"
ECOWAS Protocol on the Free Movement of Persons, Residence and Establishment	1979	Protocol to establish the free movement of people, combat human trafficking, and create harmonizing migration policies for the development of members states.
The ECOWAS General Convention on Social Security	2012	Convention to promote the equal treatment between migrant workers and nationals.
ECOWAS Child Policy	2019	Policy to protect children's rights and create a protective environment for children, free from abuse, exploitation, and violence.
ECOWAS Environmental Policy	2008	Policy for natural resource management and guidance to address environmental problems.
ECOWAS Regional Climate Strategy	2022	Strategy for action against climate change, including adaptation and mitigation efforts.
ECOWAS Protocol on the Fight Against Corruption	2001	Protocol to address and prevent corruption

With respect to human and labour rights, ECOWAS has developed several frameworks and initiatives. ECOWAS does not have its own legal instrument but refers to the provisions of the African Charter on Human and People's Rights under Article 4g of the revised ECOWAS Treaty. The ECOWAS Child Policy and Strategic Plan of Action (2019-30) as well as the Child Protection Systems Strengthening Strategic Framework in 2017 aim to end child labour in all its forms by 2025 in line with the SDGs (ECOWAS, 2019[19]). ECOWAS also set up a Gender Development Centre in 2003 and adopted a Gender Policy in 2004 to develop policies and advocacy on gender equality and to address issues such as sexual harassment in the workplace (ECOWAS, 2022[20]). Moreover, ECOWAS collaborates on the promotion of RBC with relevant human and labour rights organisations in the region, notably the Network of National Human Rights Institutions of West Africa, as well as the UN OHCHR and ILO regional offices in West Africa.

ECOWAS has lately increased its focus on climate change and the environment, but few of the relating policies and initiatives provide concrete guidance for private sector involvement. In 2008, ECOWAS adopted its Environmental Policy, which provides a common framework for natural resource management and guidance to address environmental problems. The 2022 ECOWAS Regional Climate Strategy creates a coherent basis for long-term climate action and is aligned with the African Union (AU) strategy on climate change, the Paris Agreement and the ECOWAS Vision 2050 as well as the African Union Vision 2063 (ECOWAS, 2022[21]). The strategy's action plan for 2022-30 aims among others at strengthening ECOWAS co-operation to lower GHG emissions and foresees the elaboration and implementation of a CSR policy for the ECOWAS Commission. ECOWAS has further been involved in various initiatives and partnerships to address deforestation, notably by adopting in 2013 the Convergence Plan for the Sustainable Management and Utilization of Forest Ecosystems in West Africa and by collaborating in its implementation. The plan aims to mobilise political, institutional, financial and technical support to address transboundary forest issues across the ECOWAS Member States (FAO, 2019[22]).

In the area of governance, ECOWAS has made efforts and commitments to promote and strengthen the fight against corruption. The ECOWAS Protocol on the Fight Against Corruption was adopted in 2001 and provides guidance to address and prevent acts of corruption both in the public and private sectors. Among others, each Member State is required to establish a specialised and independent anti-corruption agency. Moreover, the protocol aims to harmonise and co-ordinate national anti-corruption laws and policies (ECOWAS, 2001[23]). At the initiative of ECOWAS, the Network of National Anti-Corruption Institutions in West Africa was created in 2010, which serves as a forum for exchanges and consultation between national anti-corruption institutions in ECOWAS countries (NACIWA, n.d.[24]).

Sectoral policies and initiatives at ECOWAS level

In addition to having developed policies relevant for RBC in the areas covered by the OECD MNE Guidelines, ECOWAS has also elaborated sector-specific policies and initiatives to promote RBC in key economic sectors. Minerals and agriculture, in particular the oil, gold, cocoa beans and natural gas production are the most important sectors for the socio-economic development in West Africa contributing strongly to investment and exports (OEC, 2020[25]). These sectors and commodities are especially vulnerable to structural issues such as high rates of informal employment, conflict, child labour and deforestation.

According to the ILO, informal employment in West Africa represents over 90% (ILO, 2021[26]). For instance, informality is a prevalent issue in artisanal and small-scale gold mining, with makeshift sites created by "gold rushes" proving particularly challenging to formalise (OECD, 2022[27]). Artisanal gold has also been used to circumvent West African exchange-control regulations and the requirement to repatriate foreign currency in transnational schemes involving tax evasion, money laundering and fraud (OECD, 2018[28]; ARM, 2016[29]). Artisanal and small-scale mining has also been targeted by armed groups to extract rent and finance their operations, especially in the Sahel (ICG, 2019[30]; ISS, 2021[31]; OECD, 2020[32]). Along with informality, child labour remains prevalent in ECOWAS, in particular in the agricultural sector. In the region, 26% of children aged 5-11 were engaged in economic activity in 2020 (ILO, 2022[33]). Furthermore, environmental issues, such as deforestation are a long-standing issue closely linked to the agricultural sector (AUC/OECD, 2022[34]). For instance, the cocoa production has proven to cause forest loss and degradation of the region's biodiversity (Sassen et al., 2022[35]).

ECOWAS has recognised the responsibility to address these issues through various policies and initiatives. In the mining sector, for instance, the Directive on the Harmonization of Guiding Principles and Policies in the Mining Sector requires companies to engage local communities before and during operations in the mining, oil and gas industries as laid out in Article 16.3 (ECOWAS, 2009[36]). ECOWAS has also been engaged with the African Minerals Development Centre hosted by the AU on various policy, research and capacity-building activities to implement the Africa Mining Vision, which aims at the sustainable exploitation of mineral resources (AU, n.d.[37]). Moreover, the Inter-Governmental Action Group against Money Laundering in West Africa, an ECOWAS institution established in 1999, as well as the Liptako-Gourma Authority, created in 1970 and promoting mining and agricultural development and security co-operation in Burkina Faso, Mali and Niger have included the OECD Guidance for Responsible Mineral Supply Chains as part of their recommendations (OECD, 2018[28]).

In the agricultural sector, ECOWAS adopted a 2025 Strategic Policy Framework for its Agricultural Policy in 2017, which seeks to promote agricultural development and the sustainability of food systems in West Africa. While it does not refer to RBC directly, this framework sets out concrete objectives and targets, which relate to business conduct in the sector, notably animal health, food and nutrition security, and climate change adaptation (ECOWAS, 2022[38]; ECOWAS, 2017[39]).

The development of these regional policy frameworks and concrete targets in the minerals and agricultural sectors are an important step towards tackling adverse impacts which are linked to business conduct, such as child labour or deforestation. However, these issues continue to be highly prevalent in ECOWAS and the key challenge remains to implement and enforce concrete reforms effectively driving responsible business practices.

Policies and initiatives relevant for RBC at the national level

Beyond policies and initiatives at the regional level, ECOWAS Member States have also taken measures at the national level that are relevant for RBC. Overall, the 15 ECOWAS Member States, have adhered to several international instruments in areas covered by the OECD MNE Guidelines, such as human rights, labour rights, the environment and governance.

As shown in Table 6.2, all ECOWAS Member States have ratified key climate and governance related agreements such as the Paris Agreement, as well as the UN Convention against Corruption. However, regarding human and labour rights frameworks there remain gaps in the adherence. For instance, not all ECOWAS countries have adhered to all Core UN Conventions on Human Rights nor to all Fundamental ILO Conventions.

Beyond the adherence and ratification of international instruments, strong national policies and strategies are needed to enable and implement RBC. Over the last years, National Action Plan (NAPs) on Business and Human Rights and/or on RBC have been adopted by several countries worldwide to promote an overarching policy framework on RBC and mainstream responsible business expectations across relevant policies.

The development of NAPs in ECOWAS has been limited so far and has stemmed either from a government initiative or from a human rights institution with the support of civil society. Currently, Ghana, Nigeria and Liberia are in the process of developing a NAP (see Table 6.3). In November 2022, Ghana announced its commitment to launch a NAP by July 2023. The Commission on Human Rights and Administrative Justice and academic institutions in Ghana have engaged in conducting research, organizing multi-stakeholder dialogues and other awareness raising and capacity building efforts to help initiate a NAP process. In 2022, the Ghana Institute of Management and Public Administration (GIMPA) undertook a national baseline and gaps assessment of Business and Human Rights in Ghana in collaboration with GIMPA and the Danish

Institute for Human Rights (GIMPA, 2022[40]). In Nigeria, efforts to develop a NAP have been led by the National Human Rights Commission of Nigeria (NHRC) and civil society since 2012. A draft NAP was published in 2017. The draft NAP is a working document and anticipates that it will be updated with further inputs to reflect varying regional and geopolitical considerations within the country (NHRC, 2017[41]).

In some ECOWAS Member States the commitment to develop a NAP has been included in other government policy measures. This has been the case in Liberia. The government's Pro-Poor Agenda for Prosperity and Development, published in 2018, includes a commitment to develop and implement a NAP. The first step was to include an action point in this regard in the 2013-18 National Human Rights Action Plan (Government of Liberia, 2018[42]). In 2019, the Ministry of Justice has chaired a National Steering Committee on Business and Human Rights, which is leading the development of the NAP. The Office of the High Commissioner for Human Rights has provided support to this process in Liberia through capacity-building of stakeholders and awareness-raising activities (OHCHR, 2022[43]).

Table 6.2. Adherence/ Ratification of key international RBC-related frameworks in ECOWAS

	Core UN Conventions on Human Rights	Voluntary Principles on Security and Human Rights	Fundamental ILO Conventions	Kyoto Protocol	Paris Agreement	Convention on Biological Diversity	UN Convention against Corruption	Extractives Industries Transparency Initiative
BEN	9/9	□	8/10	■	■	■	■	□
BFA	9/9	□	9/10	■	■	■	■	■
CPV	8/9	□	9/10	■	■	■	■	□
CIV	7/9	□	10/10	■	■	■	■	■
GMB	9/9	□	8/10	■	■	■	■	□
GNB	8/9	■	8/10	■	■	■	■	■
GIN	8/9	□	9/10	■	■	■	■	■
LBR	8/9	□	7/10	■	■	■	■	□
MLI	7/9	□	8/10	■	■	■	■	■
NGA	9/9	□	9/10	■	■	■	■	■
SEN	9/9	□	10/10	■	■	■	■	■
SLE	9/9	■	10/10	■	■	■	■	■
TGO	9/9	□	10/10	■	■	■	■	■

Note: ■ = Ratified / member / developed; □ = Not ratified / not member.

Table 6.3. Development of National Action Plan on Business and Human Rights in ECOWAS

	BEN	BFA	CPV	CIV	GMB	GHA	GIN	GNB	LBR	MLI	NER	NGA	SEN	SLE	TGO
NAP under development	□	□	□	□	□	■	□	□	■	□	□	■	□	□	□

In addition to these first developments of NAPs, ECOWAS governments have different RBC-related policies and frameworks in place, notably in the extractive and agricultural sectors with respect to environmental and labour issues. For instance, in the extractive sector, most national mining codes include provisions on the protection of the environment (e.g. in Burkina Faso, Guinea, Mali, Niger, Togo). Most governments have also adopted national policies on labour issues in supply chains such as child labour and forced labour. Moreover, several ECOWAS Member States have introduced laws regarding social and environmental impact assessments of public and private investment projects, such as in Cabo Verde (FAO, 2022[44]). An overview of relevant policies across countries is listed in Annex 6.A.

Apart from national policies relating to RBC issues, ECOWAS countries, like their counterparts in other regions, have concluded several bilateral trade and investment agreements. These agreements increasingly include expectations on RBC and related areas such as human rights, climate change and sustainable development (Gaukrodger, 2021[45]). For instance, the 2016 Morocco-Nigeria bilateral investment treaty includes provisions on the protection of human rights and on CSR (Zugliani, 2019[46]; UNCTAD, 2016[47]). A further example which includes all ECOWAS Member States is the new Partnership Agreement between the EU and members of the Organisation of African, Caribbean and Pacific (ACP) States (Post-Cotonou agreement), which aims to guide the political and economic relations between EU and ACP countries. The negotiations were concluded in 2021 but the agreement has not been formally signed yet. The agreement explicitly states that signatories shall promote RBC and prioritises climate change, the environment, and sustainable development. It further references the OECD Guidelines for MNEs on RBC and the OECD Due Diligence Guidance for Responsible Supply Chains of Minerals from Conflict-Affected and High-Risk Areas as well as the UNGPs and the ILO Tripartite Declaration (EC, 2022[48]).

Access to remedy for business-related adverse impacts in ECOWAS

An essential pillar of RBC across international standards is providing access to effective remedy. As part of their duty to protect against business related adverse impacts, States are expected to take appropriate steps to ensure, through judicial, administrative, legislative or other appropriate means, that when such abuses occur within their territory and/ or jurisdiction those affected have access to effective remedy (UN-OECD-EU-ILO-SDJW, 2019[13]).

At the regional level the ECOWAS Community Court of Justice can play a role in providing access to remedy for business related adverse impacts. Operational since 2000, the Court is mandated with resolving disputes related to the ECOWAS treaty, protocols, and conventions including complaints alleging human rights violations including by businesses in the ECOWAS Member States. It can hear cases even if domestic remedies have not been exhausted, including cases still pending before the national courts, which is an exception among international tribunals. It has adjudicated several significant cases relating to business and human rights, such as the right to equal pay for equal value (Ukaigwe, 2016[49]) and is recognised as an innovative mechanism for environmental jurisprudence within Africa. For instance, the Court has ruled on a case relating to the environmental impact of oil companies in Nigeria and another case on the human rights impact of an iron ore project in Guinea (Debevoise & Plimpton, 2021[50]; ECOWAS, n.d.[51]; FES, 2022[52]; UNDP, 2022[53]). The Court is further one of the few international judicial bodies, which has explicitly cited international RBC standards in its jurisprudence, notably the UN Guiding Principles on Business and Human Rights.

Beyond this legal mechanism, a non-judicial grievance mechanism accessible for stakeholders in ECOWAS are the National Contact Points for RBC. Any trade union, civil society organisation or community can file a complaint with this mechanism for alleged violations of the OECD Guidelines for Multinational Enterprises on RBC by businesses operating in or from one of the 51 countries that have adhered to this instrument. While none of the ECOWAS Member States has adhered to the Guidelines, several cases have been filed for harm that occurred in the ECOWAS region. Between 2001 and 2022, 21 specific instances have been submitted in relation to business operations in ECOWAS host countries. Most of them concern the mining sector and are linked to environmental, human rights and employment issues.

ECOWAS stakeholders' awareness of RBC and related initiatives

In parallel to the policies and initiatives taken by ECOWAS and its Member States, businesses and civil society in the region have started to develop or participate in initiatives relevant for RBC. These actions are still at an early stage and need to be further mainstreamed. At the same time, increased uptake of RBC practices requires stronger support from governments to establish enabling policies and regulatory environments promoting RBC.

Across ECOWAS Member States, initiatives by civil society actors, and businesses have increased their focus on promoting responsible business conduct. There is a broad range of Civil Society Organisations active in ECOWAS Member States. advocating to drive forward the RBC agenda notably with respect to the environment and human rights. Some organisations have set up specific programmes to raise awareness on RBC. In Liberia, for instance, the Sustainable Development Institute works on a project to promote corporate governance and social responsibility (SDI Liberia, n.d.[54]). Moreover, several organisations are developing RBC-related projects in the mining sector such as the Wassa Association of Communities Affected by Mining in Ghana, Actions Mines Guinée in Guinea, the Fédération des Femmes Minières du Mali and Lumière Synergie pour le Développement in Senegal (see list in Annex 6.A).

Several businesses, notably in the minerals and agricultural sector, have started to engage or collaborate more actively in initiatives to promote responsible supply chains. For instance, 173 companies in the ECOWAS region are participating in the UN Global Compact regional networks, which aim to foster sustainable development in the areas of human rights, labour, environment and anti-corruption (UNGC, 2021[55]). Several companies and industry initiatives in West Africa have started programmes which aim to promote formalisation and address issues such as corruption, illicit trade, child labour and deforestation. For instance, the cocoa sector in Côte d'Ivoire and Ghana has seen an increased focus on voluntary sustainability standards, certifications and corporate initiatives implemented by a broad range of stakeholders since the mid-2000s (Ingram et al., 2018[56]; AUC/OECD, 2022[3]). In the gold mining sector in Burkina Faso, the Responsible Mining Alliance has worked directly with miners to support the creation of legal mining activities (ARM, 2019[57]). Moreover, some companies operating in ECOWAS have adopted policies aligned with the OECD due diligence framework. In Burkina Faso, Côte d'Ivoire and Mali and Niger, business and civil society representatives have already been engaged in trainings on the OECD Guidance for Responsible Mineral Supply Chains (ARM, 2022[58]).

Moreover, ECOWAS stakeholders are increasingly involved in African continental initiatives on RBC as well. For instance, various representatives from ECOWAS countries including civil society, business and trade unions participated in the first ever African Business and Human Rights Forum in Accra, Ghana in October 2022 to discuss challenges and opportunities for promoting RBC in Africa. However, the general awareness about RBC standards and due diligence approaches remains limited in the region. Case studies on the implementation of due diligence processes in minerals supply chains in Burkina Faso and Nigeria found that the level of knowledge and understanding of international due diligence frameworks and supply chain traceability was very low (BGR, 2022[59]).

While awareness about the relevance and the elements of RBC has increased among stakeholders in West Africa, ECOWAS and its Member States have set out concrete policies to promote RBC in line with international standards. Yet, there is still a way to go in the implementation and enforcement of these policies and in building the capacity of companies to carry out due diligence. This will require a joint effort between governments, business and civil society. By effectively promoting RBC, ECOWAS can seize the opportunity to strengthen sustainable value chains, to attract quality investment and to take the next steps towards sustainable development.

References

AfDB (2020), *WEST AFRICA REGIONAL INTEGRATION STRATEGY PAPER 2020-2025*, https://www.afdb.org/en/documents/west-africa-regional-integration-strategy-paper-2020-2025-0. [18]

ARM (2022), *Training program on the OECD due diligence guidance for responsible mineral supply chains from conflict-affected and high-risk areas, Alliance for Responsible Mining*, https://www.responsiblemines.org/en/project/training-due-diligence/. [58]

ARM (2019), *Support for the creation of a legal artisanal and small-scale mining (ASM) activity in Burkina Faso*, https://www.responsiblemines.org/en/project/support-for-the-creation-of-a-legal-artisanal-and-small-scale-mining-asm-activity-in-burkina-faso/. [57]

ARM (2016), *Supply Chains of Artisanal Gold in West Africa, Alliance for Responsible Mining*, https://www.responsiblemines.org/wp-content/uploads/2018/04/Publication-supply-chains-artisanal-gold-west-africa_-ENGL_-baja.pdf. [29]

Asante et al. (2022), *Foreign direct investment and economic growth nexus in ECOWAS: The leveraging effect of anti-corruption*, https://doi.org/10.20885/ejem.vol14.iss2.art3. [8]

AU (n.d.), *African Minerals Development Centre*, https://au.int/en/amdc. [37]

AUC/OECD (2022), *Africa's Development Dynamics 2022: Regional Value Chains for a Sustainable Recovery*, OECD Publishing, Paris/African Union Commission, Addis Ababa, https://doi.org/10.1787/2e3b97fd-en. [34]

AUC/OECD (2022), "Integrating value chains in West Africa and the agri-food industry", in *Africa's Development Dynamics 2022: Regional Value Chains for a Sustainable Recovery*, OECD Publishing, Paris, https://doi.org/10.1787/e68c02a0-en. [3]

BGR (2022), *The implementation of due diligence in 3TG supply chains*, https://rue.bmz.de/resource/blob/116500/fba09fda1b0e0b8b8be4f6a1b6e28568/bgr-3tg-study-2022-data.pdf. [59]

Debevoise & Plimpton (2021), *UN Guiding Principles on Business and Human Rights at 10*, https://www.ohchr.org/sites/default/files/Documents/Issues/Business/UNGPsBHRnext10/debevoise.pdf. [50]

EC (2022), *ACP-EU partnership*, https://international-partnerships.ec.europa.eu/policies/european-development-policy/acp-eu-partnership_en. [48]

EC (2022), *Corporate sustainability due diligence, European Commission*, https://commission.europa.eu/business-economy-euro/doing-business-eu/corporate-sustainability-due-diligence_en. [4]

ECOWAS (2022), *Economic Community of West Africa Agricultural Policy (ECOWAP)*, https://ecowap.ecowas.int/about-ecowap. [38]

ECOWAS (2022), *ECOWAS Gender Development Centre*, https://ccdg.ecowas.int/. [20]

ECOWAS (2022), *ECOWAS Regional Climate Strategy (RCS) And Action plan (2022-2030)*, http://www.climatestrategy.ecowas.int/images/documentation/ECOWAS%20Regional%20Climate%20Strategy_adopted%20june%202022.pdf. [21]

ECOWAS (2019), *ECOWAS Child Policy 2019-2030*, https://ecowas.int/wp-content/uploads/2022/03/ECOWAS-CHILD-POLICY-ENG-CON-Printed.pdf. [19]

ECOWAS (2018), *ECOWAS Common Investment Code*, https://wacomp.projects.ecowas.int/wp-content/uploads/2020/03/ECOWAS-COMMON-INVESTMENT-CODEENGLISH.pdf. [17]

ECOWAS (2018), *ECOWAS Investment Policy*, https://wacomp.projects.ecowas.int/wp-content/uploads/2020/03/ECOWAS-INVESTMENT-POLICY-ENGLISH.pdf. [16]

ECOWAS (2017), *2025 ECOWAP Strategic Policy Framework*, http://araa.org/sites/default/files/media/ECOWAP%202025%20Strategic%20Policy%20Framework%20ENG.pdf. [39]

ECOWAS (2009), *DIRECTIVE C/DIR.3/05/09*, http://ecowas.akomantoso.com/_lang/en-US/doc/_iri/akn/ecowas/statement/directive/2009-05-27/C_DIR.3_05_09/eng@/!main. [36]

ECOWAS (2001), *Economic Community of West African States Protocol on the Fight against Corruption*, https://eos.cartercenter.org/uploads/document_file/path/406/ECOWAS_Protocol_on_Corruption.pdf. [23]

ECOWAS (n.d.), *Import and export*, https://ecoslate.github.io/doing-business-in-ecowas/import-and-export/index.htm. [5]

ECOWAS (n.d.), *The Community Court of Justice*, https://ecowas.int/institutions/community-court-of-justice/. [51]

European Commission (2023), *Corporate social responsibility & Responsible business conduct*, European Commission, https://ec.europa.eu/growth/industry/sustainability/corporate-social-responsibility_en. [12]

FAO (2022), *FAOLEX Database, Cabo Verde. Decree-Law No. 27/2020 approving the Legal Framework for Environmental Impact Assessment (EIA).*, https://www.fao.org/faolex/results/details/en/c/LEX-FAOC194850/. [44]

FAO (2019), *Global transformation of forests for people and climate: A focus on West Africa.*, https://www.fao.org/redd/news/detail/en/c/1235031/. [22]

FES (2022), *The State of Busines and Human Rights in Africa*, https://library.fes.de/pdf-files/bueros/fes-ua/19589-20221107.pdf. [52]

Gaukrodger, D. (2021), "The future of investment treaties - possible directions", *OECD Working Papers on International Investment*, No. 2021/03, OECD Publishing, Paris, https://doi.org/10.1787/946c3970-en. [45]

GIMPA (2022), *Ghana National Baseline Assessment*, https://chraj.gov.gh/wp-content/uploads/2022/07/Baseline-Assessment-of-Business-and-Human-Rights.pdf. [40]

Government of Liberia (2018), *Pro Poor Agenda For Prospoerity And Development*, https://globalnaps.org/wp-content/uploads/2019/01/liberia-national-development-agenda-pro-poor-agenda.pdf. [42]

ICG (2019), *Getting a Grip on Central Sahel's Gold Rush, International Crisis Group*, https://icg-prod.s3.amazonaws.com/282%20Getting%20a%20Grip%20.pdf. [30]

ILO (2022), *ILOSTAT, SDG indicator 8.7.1 - Proportion of children engaged in economic activity (%) | Annual*, https://ilostat.ilo.org/data/. [33]

ILO (2021), *Employment impact assessments in Africa: Application and suitability of local multiplier analysis*, https://www.ilo.org/wcmsp5/groups/public/---ed_emp/documents/publication/wcms_835560.pdf. [26]

Ingram, V. et al. (2018), *The Impacts of Cocoa Sustainability Initiatives in West Africa*, https://doi.org/10.3390/su10114249. [56]

ISS (2021), *Preventing violent extremism in south-eastern Senegal, Institute for Security Studies*, https://issafrica.org/iss-today/preventing-violent-extremism-in-south-eastern-senegal. [31]

NACIWA (n.d.), *NACIWA*, https://naciwa.org/. [24]

NHRC (2017), *National Action Plan on Business and Human Rights*, https://globalnaps.org/wp-content/uploads/2017/11/nhr-national-action-plan.pdf. [41]

OEC (2020), *ECOWAS trade profile*, https://oec.world/en/profile/international_organization/ecowas. [25]

OECD (2023), *OECD Guidelines for Multinational Enterprises, 2023 Edition*, OECD Publishing, Paris, https://doi.org/10.1787/81f92357-en. [9]

OECD (2023), *OECD Recommendation on the Role of Government in promoting Responsible Business Conduct*, https://legalinstruments.oecd.org/en/instruments/OECD-LEGAL-0486. [15]

OECD (2022), *Natural Resource Governance and Fragility in the Sahel*, https://www.oecd.org/dac/2022_Natural_resource_governance_fragility_Sahel.pdf. [27]

OECD (2021), *Survey Results on Responsible Business Conduct in Latin America*, https://mneguidelines.oecd.org/oecd-business-survey-results-on-responsible-business-conduct-in-latin-america-and-the-caribbean.pdf. [1]

OECD (2020), *Illicit financial flows: artisanal and small-scale gold mining in Ghana and Liberia*, https://delvedatabase.org/uploads/resources/Illicit-financial-flows-Artisanal-and-Small-scale-Gold-mining-in-Ghana-and-Liberia.pdf. [32]

OECD (2018), *Gold at the crossroads - Assessment of the supply chains of gold produced in Burkina Faso, Mali and Niger*, http://mneguidelines.oecd.org/Assessment-of-the-supply-chains-of-gold-produced-in-Burkina-Faso-Mali-Niger.pdf. [28]

OECD (2018), *OECD Due Diligence Guidance for Responsible Business Conduct*, OECD Publishing, http://mneguidelines.oecd.org/OECD-Due-Diligence-Guidance-for-Responsible-Business-Conduct.pdf. [60]

OECD (2018), *OECD Due Diligence Guidance for Responsible Business Conduct*. [10]

OECD (2015), *OECD Policy Framework for Investment 2015 Edition*, OECD Publishing, Paris, https://doi.org/10.1787/9789264208667-en. [11]

OECD (n.d.), *OECD Due Diligence Policy Hub*, http://mneguidelines.oecd.org/due-diligence-policy-hub.htm. [14]

OHCHR (2022), *Business and Human Rights (BHR) Africa Project*, https://www.ohchr.org/en/business/bhr-africa. [43]

Punthakey, J. (2020), "Foreign direct investment and trade in agro-food global value chains", *OECD Food, Agriculture and Fisheries Papers*, No. 142, OECD Publishing, Paris, https://doi.org/10.1787/993f0fdc-en. [7]

Sassen et al. (2022), *Patterns of (future) environmental risks from cocoa expansion and intensification in West Africa call for context specific responses*, https://doi.org/10.1016/j.landusepol.2022.106142. [35]

SDI Liberia (n.d.), *Community Rights and Corporate Governance*, https://www.sdiliberia.org/index.php/Community-Rights-and-Corporate-Governance. [54]

Ukaigwe, J. (2016), *ECOWAS Law*, https://doi.org/10.1007/978-3-319-26233-8. [49]

UNCTAD (2016), *Morocco-Nigeria Bilateral Investment Agreement*, https://investmentpolicy.unctad.org/international-investment-agreements/treaty-files/5409/download. [47]

UNDP (2022), *A Baseline Assessment on Business and Human Rights in Africa*, https://www.undp.org/sites/g/files/zskgke326/files/2022-10/Baseline%20Assessment%20BHR%20Report%20EN%20-%20web.pdf. [53]

UNECA/ FES (2022), *The Continental Free Trade Area (CFTA) in Africa – A Human Rights Perspective*, https://www.ohchr.org/sites/default/files/Documents/Issues/Globalization/TheCFTA_A_HR_ImpactAssessment.pdf. [6]

UNGC (2021), *Un Global Compact Africa Strategy 2021-2023*, https://ungc-communications-assets.s3.amazonaws.com/docs/publications/UNGC_Mobilising%20Business%20in%20Africa_2021_2023.pdf. [55]

UN-OECD-EU-ILO-SDJW (2019), *Responsible business: key messages from international instruments*, United Nations, OECD, European Union, International Labour Organization, Social Justice Decent Work, https://mneguidelines.oecd.org/Brochure-responsible-business-key-messages-from-international-instruments.pdf. [13]

WBA (2021), *COVID-19 and Human Rights, World Benchmarking Alliance*, https://assets.worldbenchmarkingalliance.org/app/uploads/2021/02/CHBR-Covid-Study_110221_FINAL.pdf. [2]

Zugliani, N. (2019), *HUMAN RIGHTS IN INTERNATIONAL INVESTMENT LAW: THE 2016 MOROCCO–NIGERIA BILATERAL INVESTMENT TREATY*, https://doi.org/10.1017/S0020589319000174. [46]

Annex 6.A. RBC related frameworks and initiatives

National frameworks related to RBC

	Specific Frameworks/Policies Related to RBC
Benin	• **Extractive Sector:** 2006 Mining Code and Mining Taxation Title 4 Chapter 1: Obligations for Mining Titleholders • **Environment: 20**17 Decree No. 2017-332 on the organisation of environmental assessment procedures • **Climate Change:** 2016-25 Low-Carbon and Climate-Resilient Development Strategy • **Labour Standards:** 2018 Criminal Code of Benin on Child Labour, Child Trafficking, Slavery, Trafficking • **Other:** 2016 Law No. 2016-24 on the legal framework of the public-private partnership
Burkina Faso	• **Extractive Sector**: 2015 Burkina Faso Mining Code Section 2: Respect of Human Rights; Chapter 4: Hygiene, Health, and Safety at work in Mines and Quarries; Chapter 5: Preservation of the Environment • **Environment:** 2013 Law No. 006-2013/AN on the Environmental Code of Burkina Faso Article 46 and Article 102 • **Labour Standards: 20**08 Law No. 029-2008/AN on the Fight against Trafficking in Persons and Similar Practices on Child Trafficking, Slavery, Trafficking • **Agriculture: 20**18 Law No. 017-2018/AN on the Code of Agro-sylvo-pastoral fisheries and Wildlife Investments in Burkina Faso • **Other**: 2019 Law No. 038-2018/AN Investment Code
Cabo Verde	• **Extractive Sector:** 2015 Decree-Law No. 3/2015 establishing the legal framework for mineral exploration Chapter 6: Environmental Protection • **Environment:** 2020 Decree-Law No. 27/2020 approving the Legal Framework for Environmental Impact Assessment (EIA) • **Labour Standards:** 2015 Penal Code on Child Labour, Slavery, Trafficking • **Other: 20**12 Law No. 13/VIII/2012 on the Code of Investments
Côte D'Ivoire	• **Extractive Sector:** 2014 Mining Code Chapter 9: Rights and Obligations Attached to the Performance of Mining or Quarrying Operations • **Environment: 19**96 Law No. 96-766 on the Environmental Code • **Climate Change: 20**19 Côte d'Ivoire Climate-Smart Agriculture Investment Plan • **Labour Standards:** 2016 Law No. 2016-111 on the Fight Against Trafficking in Persons • **Agriculture:** 2015 Law No. 2015-537 on Agricultural Orientation of Côte d'Ivoire • **Other: 20**18 Investment Code Chapter 2: Investor Obligations (Article 36)
The Gambia	• **Extractive Sector:** 2005 Mines and Quarries Act – Act no. 7 • **Environment:** 1994 National Environment Management Act • **Climate Change:** 2021-50 The Gambia Climate Vision • **Labour Standards:** 2010 Women's Act (Act No. 12/2010) on Trafficking • **Agriculture:** 2017-26 The Agriculture and natural resources (ANR) Policy • **Other:** 2016-26 The National Entrepreneurship Policy
Ghana	• **Extractive Sector:** 2006 Minerals and Mining Act Section 18: Forestry and Environmental Protection • **Environment:** 1994 Environmental Protection Agency (EPA) Act (Act 490) • **Climate Change**: 2013 National Climate Change Policy Framework • **Labour Standards:** 1998 Children's Act on Child Labour • **Other:** 2009 Voluntary Partnership Agreement Between the European Community and the Republic of Ghana on forest law enforcement, governance and trade in timber products into the Community
Guinea	• **Extractive Sector:** 2016 Guinea Mining Code Chapter 7: Environment and Health • **Environment:** 2019 Law L/2019/0034/AN on the Environmental Code • **Labour Standards:** 2008 Children's Code of Guinea (Law No. L/2008/011/AN) on Child Labour and Child Trafficking • **Agriculture:** 2018-25 National Plan for Agricultural Investment and Food and Nutritional Security • **Other:** 2007 Corporate Social Responsibility Policy Letter and Local Content Policy Letter in the Mining sector
Guinea-Bissau	• **Extractive Sector:** 2014 Mining and Quarrying Code Section 2: Preservation of the Environment • **Environment:** 2017 Decree No. 7/2017 approving the Regulation on the Environmental and Social Impact Assessment • **Labour Standards:** 2011 Law to Prevent and Combat Human Trafficking • **Other:** 2011 Law no. 3/2011 Investment Code
Liberia	• **Extractive Sector:** 2014 Mining and Quarry Code Section 2: Preservation of the Environment; Sector 3: Hygiene and Safety • **Environment: 20**02 Environment Protection and Management Law • **Climate Change:** 2018 National Policy and Response Strategy on Climate Change • **Labour Standards:** 2015 Decent Work Act Liberia on Child Labour, Child Trafficking, Forced Labour, Other, Slavery • **Other: 20**15 Sustainable Fisheries Partnership Agreement between the European Union and the Republic of Liberia
Mali	• **Extractive Sector:** 2019 Mining Code Chapter 4: Hygiene, Health, and Security; Chapter 5: Environment and Cultural Heritage Protection; Chapter 6: Community Development

	2 015 Hydrocarbon Code Chapter 3: Environment, hygiene, health, safety and cultural heritage • **Environment: 20**13 Interministerial Order No. 2013-0256-MEA-MATDAT-SG setting the terms of public consultation on Environmental and Social Impact Assessment • **Climate Change:** 2011 National Policy on Climate Change • **Labour Standards:** 2002 Child Protection Code • **Agriculture: 20**19 Climate-Smart Agriculture Investment Plan • **Other:** 2018 Law No. 2018-033 relating to fraudulent commercial practices
Niger	• **Extractive Sector:** 2007 Mining Code Article 99: Mine or quarry substances mining and the environment 2 019 Petroleum Policy E.7 Environmental and Social Impacts • **Environment: 20**18 Law No. 2018-28 on the fundamental principles of Environmental Assessment • **Climate Change:** 1998 Law no. 98-56 (Framework Law on Environmental Management) • **Labour Standards:** 2012 Decree No. 2012-082 / PRN / MJ on Child Labour and Forced Labour • **Agriculture: 20**10 Ordinance No. 2010-29 on pastoralism • **Other: 20**14 Law 2014-09 Investment Code Chapter 2: Obligations
Nigeria	• **Extractive Sector:** 2007 The Nigerian Extractive Industries Transparency Initiative Act 2 006 National Oil Spill Detection and Response Agency Act • **Environment: 19**92 Environmental Impact Assessment Act • **Climate Change: 20**21 Climate Change Act • **Labour Standards:** 2003 Child's Right Act on Child Labour, Forced Labour, and Slavery • **Other: 20**11 Nigerian Securities and Exchange Commission Code of Corporate Governance for Public Companies 2 012 Implementation of Sustainable Banking Principles by banks, discount houses, and development finance institutions in Nigeria
Senegal	• **Extractive Sector:** 2019 Law No. 2019-03 Petroleum Code • **Environment:** 2001 Decree No. 2001-282 on the Environmental Code • **Climate Change:** 2020 The Senegal Investment Climate Reform Action Plan • **Labour Standards:** 1997 Labour code (Law No. 97-17) on Forced Labour • **Other:** 2020-24 National Strategy for the fight against corruption
Sierra Leone	• **Extractive Sector:** 2009 The Mines and Minerals Act Part 15: Protection of the Environment; Part 16: Community Development; Part 17: Health and Safety • **Environment:** 2010 Environment Protection Agency (Environmental Impact Assessment Licence) • **Labour Standards:** 2005 Anti-Human Trafficking Act on Child Trafficking and Forced Labour • **Other:** 2008 Anti-Corruption Act
Togo	• **Extractive Sector:** 1996 Mining Code Article 34: Protection of the Environment 2 011 Law No. 2011-008 on the contribution of mining companies to the local and regional development • **Environment:** 2022-29 Decree No. 2016-007/PR On management bodies for the reduction of greenhouse gas emissions due to deforestation and forest degradation (REDD+) • **Climate Change:** 2018 National Adaptation Plan on Climate Change • **Labour Standards:** 2015 Penal Code on Child Trafficking, Forced Labour, Slavery, and Trafficking • **Other: 20**19 Law No. 2019-005 on the Investment Code
Regional/ Continental	• **Extractive Sector:** 2009 Directive C/DIR.3/5/09 on the harmonisation of guiding principles and policies for the mining sector of ECOWAS • **Environment: 19**68 African Convention on the Conservation of Nature and Natural Resources (revised 2013) • **Labour Standards: 20**20 African Union Ten Year Action Plan to Eradicate Child Labour, Forced Labour, Human Trafficking and Modern Slavery (2020- 2030) 1 990 African Union Charter on the Rights and Welfare of the Child • **Other: 20**03 African Convention on Preventing and Combating Corruption 2 016 Pan-African Investment Code Article 22: Corporate Social Responsibility; Article 24: Business Ethics and Human Rights; Article 34: Labor Issues; Article 37: Environment

CSOs working on RBC related issues

Country	Organisation	Website	RBC related programmes
Benin	Nature Tropicale ONG	www.naturetropicale.org	Environment, climate change
	La Dynamique OSCAF		
Burkina Faso	Optimum Travail du Burkina		
Côte d'Ivoire	Groupe de Recherche et de Plaidoyer sur les Industries Extractives		
Ghana	Center for Indigenous Knowledge and Organizational Development	https://cikodgh.com/	Indigenous Rights, sustainable development and agriculture

	Livelihood and Environment Ghana		
	Wassa Association of Communities Affected by Mining	http://www.wacamgh.org/	Human Rights, environment, mining
	Strategic Youth Network Development		
Guinea	Centre de Commerce International pour le Développement		
	Actions Mines Guinee	https://actionminesguinee.org/	Mining, sustainable development
Libera	Committee for Peace and Development Advocacy		
	Green Advocates		
	Sustainable Development Institute	https://sdiliberia.org/	Natural resource management, corporate governance and social responsibility
Mali	African Mining Alliance		
	Fondation pour le développement au Sahel		
	Fédération des Femmes Minières du Mali		
Niger	Collectif des Organisations de Défense des Droits de L'Homme et de la Démocratie		
Nigeria	African Law Foundation		
	Civil Society Legislative Advocacy Centre		
	Community Enhancement and Environmental Awareness Foundation		
	Community Policing Partners for Justice, Security and Democratic Reforms		
	Environmental Rights Action		
	Foundation For Environmental Rights, Advocacy & Development		
	Foundation for the Conservation of the Earth		
	Global Rights Nigeria	https://www.globalrights.org/ng/	Human Rights, governance, business and human rights
	Leadership Initiative for Transformation and Empowerment		
	Peace Point Development Foundation		
	Support Initiative for Sustainable Development		
Senegal	Lumière Synergie pour le Développement	www.lsdsenegal.org	Mining, sustainable development
	Enda Lead Afrique Francophone		
Sierra Leone	Community Advocacy and Development Movement		
	Network Movement for Justice & Development		
	Women's Center for Good Governance and Human Rights		
Togo	ONG Dimension Humaine		
	Programme d'Appui à la Femme et à l'Enfance Déshéritée		
	Association pour l'Auto-promotion des communautes de Base		